# Techniques in the Clinical Supervision of Teachers

## Preservice and Inservice Applications

## Second Edition

**Keith A. Acheson**

**Meredith Damien Gall**

University of Oregon

Longman

New York & London

Executive Editor: Raymond T. O'Connell
Production Editor: Halley Gatenby
Cover Design: Joseph DePinho
Text Art: J & R Services, Inc.
Production Supervisor: Judith Stern
Compositor: Graphicraft Typesetters Ltd.
Printer and Binder: The Alpine Press

**Techniques in the Clinical Supervision of Teachers,** Second Edition

Longman Inc.
95 Church Street
White Plains, N.Y. 10601

Associated companies:
Longman Group Ltd., London
Longman Cheshire Pty., Melbourne
Longman Paul Pty., Auckland
Copp Clark Pitman, Toronto
Pitman Publishing Inc., New York

**Library of Congress Cataloging-in-Publication Data**

Acheson, Keith A., 1925–
    Techniques in the clinical supervision of teachers.

    Bibliography
    Includes index.
    1. Student teaching. 2. Teachers—In-service
training. 3. School supervision. 4. Observation
(Educational method) 5. Teachers' workshops.
I. Gall, Meredith D., 1942–    . II. Title.
LB2157.A3A29 1987      371.1'46      86-2883
ISBN 0-582-28563-1

88 89 90     9 8 7 6 5 4 3

# Contents

# Acknowledgments

Some of the ideas in this book were developed at Stanford University in the early 1960s along with techniques for using videotape and other forms of feedback in the training of preservice and inservice teachers. People in that project who influenced the ideas, research, and applications were Robert Bush, Dwight Allen, Fred McDonald, Norman Boyan, Horace Aubertine, Bill Johnson, Jim Olivero, Frank MacGraw, Al Robertson, and Jimmy Fortune.

Both authors, along with John Hansen, worked on earlier versions of the techniques presented here as part of a project sponsored by the Far West Laboratory for Educational Research and Development. The support and suggestions of Walter Borg and Ned Flanders were especially helpful. The materials that grew out of the project were used in many workshops and were published by the Association of California School Administrators and, later, at Florida State University. Ed Beaubier and Art Thayer were instrumental during this phase of the materials' development, as was Ray Hull.

For the past decade, research conducted at the University of Oregon by the authors, their colleagues, and students has influenced the attitudes and recommendations reflected in the book. We thank Peter Titze, Wes Tolliver, Michael Carl, Colin Yarham, Gary Martin, Jim Shinn, Judy Aubrecht, John Suttle, and Kathy Lovell. Several professional associations and state education departments have supported the development and dissemination of the ideas and procedures recounted here. We are especially grateful to the Confederation of Oregon School Administrators and Ozzie Rose, the Oregon State Department of Education and Ron Burge, the Nevada Association of School Administrators, the principals' and superintendents' associations in Washington State and British Columbia, the Nebraska Association for Supervision and Curriculum Development, the British

Columbia Ministry of Education and Russ Leskiw, the National Academy of School Executives, and the many school districts that have conducted workshops and conferences using our materials and personnel.

The research of Dale Bolton at the University of Washington and Rob Spaulding at San Jose State has influenced our conclusions. Reports of our work have been presented at two conventions of the American Educational Research Association, in a paper written in collaboration with Paul Tucker and Cal Zigler, and, more recently, in a symposium with members of the Teacher Corps Research Adaptation Cluster. We also thank the administrators and teachers who reacted to earlier drafts of the materials in three annual workshops conducted on Orcas Island in Washington State.

Since publication of the first edition of this book, the authors, our students, and our colleagues have continued to conduct research, interact with people in the field, and consider trends in supervision. What we see—not only in the United States but in other countries as well—is a movement toward the kind of processes we described in the first edition. This new edition adds material on teacher evaluation, collegial observation, research, and other aspects of supervision that are growing in importance.

We thank those people with whom we have worked in Alberta, British Columbia, Manitoba, and Saskatchewan, Canada; in Australia, Guam, Japan, Jordan, Mexico, Saudi Arabia, Singapore, and South Korea; and in Alaska, the District of Columbia, Kansas, Montana, Oregon, and Washington State.

The number of individuals to thank has grown geometrically; the number of annual workshops conducted on Orcas Island in Washington State has proceeded arithmetically—to 10 at the time of this writing. The participants have reacted to, enriched, and improved our expanding ideas.

# A Note to the Instructor

The content of this book can be taught in several formats. We recommend taking up observation techniques as early as possible, giving the participants opportunities to practice in a live setting whenever possible and to share experiences and data with other class members. Planning conferences can be introduced as a topic related to trying out different observation systems. An analysis of a planning conference is a reasonable assignment. Teachers should be selected for their willingness to let observers practice their skills. Observers who have student teachers assigned to them and principals who have a faculty to work with should have no difficulty finding opportunities to apply their new skills. After feedback conferences have been discussed, students should have a chance to work through several complete cycles with a teacher.

Simulated situations can be set up to allow participants to practice observing short lessons taught by classmates to their peers. Participants can also practice conference skills in role-playing sessions with classmates, using data supplied by the instructor; an observer for each pair of role players allows for subsequent debriefing and discussion. Tape recordings of conferences are useful in the analysis process, but we find that many teachers are reluctant to permit tape recording unless they understand clearly what use will be made of the tapes and that they will not be evaluated or embarrassed in the process.

A number of activities, exercises, and assignments can be used in conjunction with the printed materials and instructor presentations. Listing what class members feel to be the crucial competencies of teaching will stimulate interest in the aspects of teaching effectiveness discussed in chapter 2.

Tape recordings of classroom interaction can be used to practice writing selected verbatim comments, questions, or responses. Films or videotapes showing nonverbal behaviors also can be useful. A pre-pared tape (or psychodrama) of a conference gives class members something tangible to react to when studying conference techniques. Overhead projector transparencies of data from seating charts or other observation instruments can serve as a focus for analysis and discussion.

Teaching the skills for coding interaction requires some structured practice. We suggest using a tape recording that has been carefully coded by an expert so that class members can be given feedback when they practice.

Instructor presentations on topics such as research on teaching or supervision or teacher evaluation can augment the material on these topics in this book. Small-group discussions in which participants share their experiences, data, and opinions have been valuable activities in our courses.

# A Note to the Reader

This book is about the clinical supervision of teachers. Several texts on clinical supervision have been published in the last 15 years, but in general they have emphasized theory and research on clinical supervision. Our book is practical. We emphasize the techniques of clinical supervision—the "nuts and bolts" of how to work with teachers to help them improve their classroom teaching.

In preparing the text, we were guided by a set of objectives to help you, the supervisor, develop

- an understanding of the three phases of clinical supervision: planning conference, classroom observation, and feedback conference;
- knowledge and skill in using specific techniques in conferences with teachers and in observing their classroom teaching;
- understanding of issues and problems in clinical supervision;
- understanding of role differences of the supervisor as facilitator, evaluator, counselor, and curriculum adviser;
- a positive attitude toward clinical supervision as a method of promoting teacher growth; and
- insights into the roles that teachers and principals can play in using the techniques of clinical supervision.

The textbook format is better suited for helping you to attain knowledge and for understanding objectives than it is for helping you to achieve skill-related objectives. If you are typical of most educators, you did not learn how to teach by reading textbooks. You learned how to teach by practicing the act of teaching in actual classroom situations. (We hope you had a skillful supervisor to assist you!) Textbooks may have facilitated this process by suggesting specific techniques for you to try.

The same principle applies to acquiring skill as a clinical supervisor. We would like to think that this textbook is sufficient to train you to be a highly skilled supervisor. Our experience suggests otherwise. You will need to practice and receive feedback on each conference and observation technique if you are to incorporate them into your supervisory repertoire. It will help, too, if you have the opportunity to observe supervisors who can demonstrate these techniques.

Building principals, school district personnel, and teacher educators in colleges and universities may be required to do teacher supervision as part of their duties. These professional educators need to be skilled in the processes of clinical teacher supervision. If you currently supervise teachers or if you plan to do so in the future, this book was written with you in mind.

The book is organized into five units. Unit I provides background necessary for understanding techniques of clinical supervision. Unit II deals with setting goals for a series of observations and planning for individual observations. Units III and IV describe specific techniques for collecting observation data and conducting feedback conferences. Unit V includes some speculation about the future roles of principals, teachers as instructional leaders, and more, including questions you may not have asked yet, and answers you may not be ready for. (Like the child who asked, "Ma, what's a penguin?" "Ask your father." "I don't want to know *that* much about penguins!")

# Unit I

# Introduction to Clinical Supervision

## Overview

Clinical supervision has as its goal the professional development of teachers, with an emphasis on improving teachers' classroom performance. Chapter 1 introduces you to the basic characteristics of clinical supervision and compares it with other forms of teacher supervision. As the goal of clinical supervision is effective teaching, chapter 2 presents criteria of effective teaching proposed by educators and teachers. Supervisor and teacher can use these criteria to define for themselves what is meant by "effective teaching." Chapter 3 addresses the relationship between clinical supervision and teacher evaluation.

## Objectives

The purpose of this unit is to help you develop:

Understanding of the basic processes and goals of clinical supervision.

Understanding of why teachers traditionally have had negative attitudes toward supervision.

Understanding of how clinical supervision differs from other forms of teacher supervision.

Understanding of the relationship between clinical supervision and teacher evaluation.

Knowledge about the current state of research on clinical supervision's effectiveness.

Understanding of different perspectives from which to define effective teaching.

Knowledge about criteria of effective teaching that have been discovered through research.

Skill in defining what is meant by effective teaching.

Understanding of how clinical supervision fits into a total system of formative and summative evaluation.

# 1

# The Nature of
# Clinical Supervision

## An Example

What gripes me about this so-called supervision is that the
principal only comes into my classroom once a year for about an
hour. It's a scary, unpleasant experience. I wouldn't mind if I
was being supervised by someone who's been a success in the
classroom; but usually it's someone who was a poor teacher
who's been pushed into an administrative position; and, to top
it off, that person usually has had no training whatsoever in
how to supervise.—*From a conversation with a sixth-grade teacher*

The spirit of clinical supervision is difficult to capture in words.
Clinical supervision is a process, a distinctive style of relating to
teachers. For this process to be effective, the clinical supervisor's
mind, emotions, and actions must work together to achieve the
primary goal of clinical supervision: the professional development of
the preservice or inservice teacher.

Although we acknowledge the unitary nature of clinical supervision, our book is primarily analytical. It attempts to tease out and
describe the components and techniques of clinical supervision. This
analytical approach is useful as an instructional device, but it does
not allow you to view clinical supervision as a whole. As a way of
dealing with this problem, we present an episode from an actual
case of clinical supervision.

Arthur Harris, a university supervisor, was assigned to supervise
Jim, a student teacher at a local junior high school. Harris had an
initial meeting with Jim to get acquainted, discuss the supervisory

role, and answer questions. He then met with the two teachers in whose classrooms Jim would work and with the school's principal. The two teachers gave Jim several weeks to observe their classes, become acquainted with the students, and prepare several social studies units.

Arthur Harris viewed his initial role as providing support and encouragement to Jim. Once Jim had found his bearings, Harris explained the procedures of clinical supervision and initiated a supervisory cycle by asking Jim to state his lesson plan for the class on Africa that Harris would observe later in the week. Jim's plan was to organize the students into three groups and have each group read a different article about Rhodesia. Then Jim wanted students in each group to state what they learned from the articles and answer questions about them.

Supervisor Harris and Jim agreed that it would be helpful to collect data on verbal interaction patterns in the lesson. Two specific areas of focus were selected: (1) Jim's responses to students' answers and ideas, which Harris would record using selective verbatim (technique 9), and (2) the distribution of student talk during the lesson, which would be recorded on a seating chart (technique 12).

Exhibit 1.1 shows a sample of the data collected by Arthur Harris using each technique. When Jim and Harris met the following week for a feedback conference, Jim was able to use the data to reach his own conclusions about how the lesson went. Supervisor Harris initiated this process by asking, "What do these data tell you about your teaching?" (technique 23). Jim realized that he had not praised or elaborated on student ideas other than simply to acknowledge them. Also, Jim saw that he was successful in getting students to talk, but the distribution of talk was unbalanced: students nearest the teacher, and one student in particular, did most of the speaking.

Arthur Harris's next move in the feedback conference was to ask Jim how he would explain why these verbal patterns occurred (technique 24). Jim commented that he had heard in his methods courses about the importance of responding constructively to student ideas, but he had not made the connection to his own teaching behavior until now. As for the distribution of student talk, Jim stated he was simply unaware that the imbalance had occurred. He realized, though, that he probably called a number of times on the student who talked the most because he could depend on her to give good answers.

Supervisor Harris asked Jim what he might do based on these observations (technique 25). Jim said he would practice using praise

T: Do u know what was being discussed in this article?

S: No.

T: Well, in 1984... backfire from all this ... Do u understand what that will mean?

S: —

S: —

T: that's true. OK. We know Russia is 1 of leading producers of chromium. What do we use chromium for?

S: Automobiles

S: Makes things shine

T: OK. Russia... What wld that mean?

S: We'd be...

T: OK.

S: And they'd use that against us.

T: Another thing in the article that was important?

S: Blacks CAN vote... Not many do.

T: Not many do. Do you get feeling for how blacks in Rhodesia...

Exhibit 1.1. Selective verbatim and seating chart in lesson on Africa

in his next lessons and would make an effort to call on more students. Harris suggested several ways that Jim might acknowledge student ideas and incorporate them in the lesson. He also suggested that a different arrangement of desks—perhaps a semi-circle or circle—might encourage students to express more ideas and engage in discussion among themselves.

This brief example illustrates the three phases of the clinical supervision cycle: planning conference, classroom observation, and feedback conference. The example also makes clear that clinical supervision focuses on the teacher's actual classroom performance and includes the teacher as an active participant in the supervisory process. To see what teachers want supervisors to do, study figures 1.1, 1.2, and 1.3.

## The "Problem" of Teacher Supervision

Most teachers do not like to be supervised, even though it is a required part of their training and professional work. They react defensively to supervision, and they do not find it helpful.

This generalization undoubtedly has exceptions. Some teachers profit from supervision, and some gifted supervisors are popular and effective in working with teachers. Yet the weight of evidence supports the generalization. In a study of 2500 teachers, Wiles found that only a small fraction of them (1.5 percent) perceived their supervisor as a source of new ideas.[1] Cogan conducted several studies of teacher supervision, on the basis of which he concluded that "psychologically [supervision] is almost inevitably viewed as an active threat to the teacher, possibly endangering his professional standing and undermining his confidence."[2] Blumberg reviewed studies of teacher supervision conducted by himself and others and found that teachers view supervision "as a part of the system that exists but that does not play an important role in their professional lives, almost like an organizational ritual that is no longer relevant."[3]

The prevalence of teacher hostility to supervision would suggest that schools abandon it entirely. A more hopeful conclusion is that teachers are hostile, not to supervision, but to the style of supervision they typically receive. *Teachers might react positively to a supervisory style that is more responsive to their concerns and aspirations.* Clinical supervision is based on this premise.

Before describing what clinical supervision is, let us examine some supervisory practices to which teachers react negatively. In traditional inservice supervision, the supervisor—usually the school principal—initiates the supervisory process to evaluate the teacher's performance. The evaluation function may be mandated by state

1. Meets prior to visit
2. Finds teacher objectives
3. Finds expectations of students
4. Finds teacher concerns
5. Involves T in choosing methods
6. Identifies expected behavior
7. Suggests observation techniques
8. Suggests self-supervision
9. Makes verbatim notes
10. Writes teacher's questions
11. Writes student responses
12. Records task analysis
13. Charts student responses
14. Makes audio recordings
15. Charts physical movements
16. Makes video recordings
17. Observes problem child
18. Records subjective feelings
19. Stays for thirty minutes
20. Meets after visit
21. Gives direct advice
22. Gives opinions
23. Relates T's perceptions
24. Encourages T inferences
25. Clarifies with questions
26. Encourages alternatives
27. Accommodates T's priorities
28. Listens more than talks
29. Acknowledges T's comments
30. Gives praise and encouragement
31. Recommends resources

**Figure 1.1. Actual and ideal behaviors as judged by teachers of trained (dotted lines) and untrained (solid lines) principals. From James L. Shinn, "Teacher Perceptions of Ideal and Actual Supervisory Procedures Used by California Elementary Principals" (Ph.D. diss., University of Oregon, 1976), p. 52.**

law, as in California, Oregon, and Washington, or by the local school board, or by ministries of education.

This situation creates two problems at the start. First, supervision becomes equated with evaluation. People tend to be anxious when they know they are being evaluated, especially if negative evalua-

1.  Meets prior to visit
2.  Finds teacher objectives
3.  Finds expectations of students
4.  Finds teacher concerns
5.  Involves T in choosing methods
6.  Identifies expected behavior
7.  Suggests observation techniques
8.  Suggests self-supervision
9.  Makes verbatim notes
10. Writes teacher's questions
11. Writes student responses
12. Records task analysis
13. Charts student responses
14. Makes audio recordings
15. Charts physical movements
16. Makes video recordings
17. Observes problem child
18. Records subjective feelings
19. Stays for thirty minutes
20. Meets after visit
21. Gives direct advice
22. Gives opinions
23. Relates T's perceptions
24. Encourages T inferences
25. Clarifies with questions
26. Encourages alternatives
27. Accommodates T's priorities
28. Listens more than talks
29. Acknowledges T's comments
30. Gives praise and encouragement
31. Recommends resources

**Figure 1.2.   Supervisor behavior at the present and in the future as perceived by teachers (solid lines); actual and ideal supervisor behavior as perceived by supervisors (dotted lines). From Saad Adwani, "The Relationship between Teacher and Supervisor as Perceived by Teachers, Supervisors and Principals in Secondary Schools in Saudi Arabia" (Ph.D. diss., University of Oregon, 1981), p. 184, and Saleh Al-Tuwaijri, "The Relationship between Ideal and Actual Supervisory Practice as Perceived by Supervisors in Saudi Arabia" (Ph.D. diss., University of Oregon, 1985), p. 159.**

Figure 1.3. **Behaviors before and after adopting a mandated program as judged by the evaluators. From Keith A. Acheson, Assessment of Teacher Evaluation Process 1980–81 School Year (Cottage Grove, OR: South Lane School District), pp. 21–23.**

tions threaten their jobs. No wonder, then, that teachers react negatively to supervision. The second problem is that supervision arises from a need of the supervisor, rather than from a need felt by the teacher.

*lack of communication*

*Planning) Systematic data*

Because traditional supervision tends to be unpleasant, interaction between supervisor and teacher is avoided or minimized. Unfortunately, this practice compounds the problem. The supervisor may show up unannounced at the teacher's classroom to observe what is happening. The teacher has no knowledge of what the supervisor might observe and evaluate. Is the supervisor interested in the neatness of the classroom, in the students' apparent interest in their work, in the objectives and teaching strategy of the lesson, or perhaps in the degree to which classroom control is maintained? The supervisor, on the other hand, may not have planned what to observe and evaluate. The result is that classroom observation data are likely to be unsystematic, highly subjective, and vague.

The follow-up to classroom visitation is not likely to improve matters. Typically the supervisor completes a rating checklist and writes an evaluative report on the teacher's performance. The teacher may not have an opportunity to confer with the supervisor about the observational data and evaluative criteria used in the report, even though the report may be used in important decisions relating to the teacher's promotion and tenure.

*Supervis vs. inspectors*

This highly directive form of supervision reflects the historical role of supervisors as school "inspectors." As far back as the early eighteenth century, lay committees in Boston were charged with inspecting schools periodically. The purpose of inspection was to determine whether instructional standards were being maintained. School inspection by lay committees continued until schools grew large enough to require more than one teacher in each school. The inspection function then became the responsibility of one of the teachers, who was known as the "principal teacher." Eventually the title was shortened to "principal." Although other models of supervision have been advocated in recent years, many principals probably still perceive their supervisory role as that of inspector.

## Clinical Supervision—A Definition

The preceding description of teacher supervision is overdrawn, yet it characterizes what some supervisors do some of the time. To the extent that the portrayal is accurate, it accounts for teachers' pervasive negative feelings about supervision. We wish to promote an alternative model of supervision that is interactive rather than directive, democratic rather than authoritarian, teacher-centered

*✳ Interactive, democratic, teacher centered*

rather than supervisor-centered. This supervisory style is called clinical supervision.

We use the label *clinical supervision* because the model presented here is based directly on the methods developed by Morris Cogan, Robert Goldhammer, and others at the Harvard School of Education in the 1960s.[4] "Clinical" is meant to suggest a face-to-face relationship between teacher and supervisor and a focus on the teacher's actual behavior in the classroom. As Goldhammer puts it, "Given close observation, detailed observational data, face-to-face interaction between the supervisor and teacher, and an intensity of focus that binds the two together in an intimate professional relationship, the meaning of 'clinical' is pretty well filled out."[5]

The word "clinical" can also connote pathology, a connotation that should not be applied to the model of teacher supervision presented here. We certainly do not wish you to think that clinical supervision is always a "remedy" applied by the supervisor to deficient or unhealthy behavior exhibited by the teacher. To avoid this implied meaning of clinical supervision, we considered using the term *teacher-centered supervision*. One nice feature of this label is that it parallels the method of "person-centered counseling" popularized by Carl Rogers,[6] with which clinical supervision has much in common. Nevertheless, we settled on "clinical supervision" as more descriptive because it continues the tradition of the group at Harvard who originated this model of supervision.

Clinical supervision acknowledges the need for teacher evaluation, under the condition that the teacher participates with the supervisor in this process. The primary emphasis of clinical supervision is on professional development, however. *It is supervision to help the teacher improve his or her instructional performance.*

How is this goal to be accomplished? The supervisor begins the process of supervision by holding a conference with the teacher. In the conference the teacher has an opportunity to state personal concerns, needs, and aspirations. The supervisor's role is to help the teacher clarify these perceptions so that the two of them have a clear picture of the teacher's current instruction, the teacher's view of ideal instruction, and whether there is a discrepancy between the two. Next, supervisor and teacher explore new techniques that the teacher might try in order to move the instruction toward the ideal.

This first phase of supervision, done properly, can be helpful to the teacher. Teaching is a lonely profession. Most teachers (i.e., those who do not work in a team teaching context) are deprived of access to colleagues with whom they can share perceptions. Supervision can satisfy this important need of teachers.

The planning conference also provides teachers with an opportunity to reflect on their teaching. Many teachers have a vague anxiety about the effectiveness of their teaching. They do not know whether they are doing a good job, whether a "problem" student can be helped, whether their instruction can be improved. Teachers rarely have the opportunity to observe other teachers' classroom performance, which might provide a basis for reflecting on their own performance. Supervisors can meet this need by using a different approach—helping the teacher clarify goals, collecting observational data on classroom events, and analyzing the data for discrepancies. For teachers who are not aware of their goals or how they "come across" in the classroom, this process can be a useful guide.

The planning conference often results in a cooperative decision by teacher and supervisor to collect observational data. For example, a teacher we know had a vaguely defined concern that he was turning off the brighter students in the class. In the planning conference the teacher developed the hypothesis that perhaps he was spending the majority of his time with the slower students in the class and ignoring the needs of the brighter students. Together, teacher and supervisor decided that it might be helpful to do a verbal flow analysis (technique 12) of the teacher's discussion behavior. This analysis involves observation of the students with whom the teacher initiates interaction and how he responds to each student's ideas. The teacher and the supervisor also decided it would be worthwhile for the teacher to collect class assignments over a two-week period to determine their level of difficulty and challenge.

It is curious how rarely we collect data on different aspects of the teacher's classroom performance. In the field of sports, for example, the athlete watches closely the statistical data that summarize observations of his performance—number of home runs in baseball, percentage of completed passes in football, final and intermediate times in track events, and so forth. Also, athletes are exposed constantly to videotape replays of their performance so that they can perfect their techniques. In professions such as medicine, business, and law, the practitioner has access to a number of indicators that directly reflect quality of performance—number of lives saved, salary based on fees, sales figures. Additionally, practitioners often hear expressions of satisfaction or dissatisfaction from their clients.

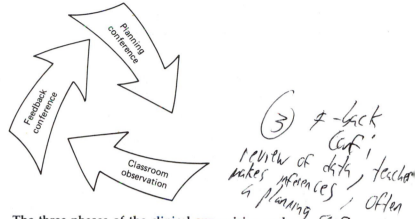

Figure 1.4.   **The three phases of the clinical supervision cycle**

③ f—back
conf;
review of data, teacher
makes inferences;
→ planning
conf, too
often

*We need to provide teachers with similar indicators of performance, based on direct or indirect observation.*

The final phase of clinical supervision is for teacher and supervisor to participate in a feedback conference. Together they review the observational data, with the supervisor encouraging the teacher to make his or her own inferences about teaching effectiveness. For example, in viewing a videotape of their performance, teachers usually notice a number of areas in which they need to improve. They comment that they hadn't known how much they talk in class, that they tend to ignore or fail to acknowledge student comments, that they do not speak forcefully enough, and the like.

As the teacher reviews the observational data, the feedback conference often turns into a planning conference—with teacher and supervisor deciding cooperatively to collect further observational data or plan a self-improvement program.

In brief, clinical supervision is a model of supervision that contains three phases: planning conference, classroom observation, and feedback conference. The model is shown graphically in figure 1.4. The most distinctive features of clinical supervision are its emphases on direct teacher-supervisor interaction and the teacher's professional development.

Richard Weller has offered a formal definition of clinical supervision: "Clinical supervision may be defined as supervision focused upon the improvement of instruction by means of systematic cycles of planning, observation, and intensive intellectual analysis of actual teaching performances in the interest of rational modification."[7]

*  direct teach-sup interaction &
emphasis on teachers prof. dev.

In addition to providing this succinct but accurate definition, Weller isolated the essential characteristics and assumptions of clinical supervision as described in the literature. An adaptation of this list of characteristics and assumptions is presented below. The characteristics are operationalized in the set of conference and observation techniques presented in chapters 4 through 11.

### Essential Characteristics and Assumptions of Clinical Supervision[8]

1. To improve instruction teachers must learn specific intellectual and behavioral skills.
2. The supervisor should take responsibility for helping the teachers to develop:

   skills for analyzing the instructional process based on systematic data;

   skills for experimentation, adaptation, and modification of the curriculum;

   a broader repertoire of teaching skills and techniques.
3. The supervisor emphasizes what and how teachers teach: to improve instruction, not change the teacher's personality.
4. The planning and analysis center on making and testing instructional hypotheses based on observational evidence.
5. The conferences deal with a few instructional issues that are important, relevant to the teacher, and amenable to change.
6. The feedback conference concentrates on constructive analysis and the reinforcement of successful patterns rather than on the condemnation of unsuccessful patterns.
7. It is based on observational evidence, not on unsubstantiated value judgments.
8. The cycle of planning, observation, and analysis is continuous and cumulative.
9. Supervision is a dynamic process of give-and-take in which supervisors and teachers are colleagues in search of mutual educational understanding.
10. The supervisory process is primarily centered on the analysis of instruction.
11. The individual teacher has both the freedom and the responsibility to initiate issues, analyze and improve his or her own teaching, and develop a personal teaching style.
12. Supervision can be perceived, analyzed, and improved in much the same manner as teaching can.
13. The supervisor has both the freedom and the responsibility to

analyze and evaluate his or her own supervision in a manner similar to a teacher's analysis and evaluation of his or her instruction.

## The Goals of Clinical Supervision

Planning conferences, classroom observation, and feedback conferences are the major activities of clinical supervision. The major aim of these activities is the improvement of teachers' classroom instruction. In this respect clinical supervision is a key technique for promoting the professional development of teachers.

The aim of clinical supervision can be analyzed into more specific goals as follows:

*To Provide Teachers with Objective Feedback on the Current State of Their Instruction.* Clinical supervision, in its most basic form holds up a mirror so that teachers can see what they are actually doing while teaching. What teachers are doing may be quite different from what teachers think they are doing. For example, many teachers believe they are good at encouraging students to express their ideas until they listen to audiotapes of their lessons. Then they discover the extent to which they dominate the lesson. Typically, two-thirds of classroom talk is by the teacher. Receiving objective feedback is often sufficient stimulus for teachers to initiate a self-improvement process.

*To Diagnose and Solve Instructional Problems.* Clinical supervisors use conference techniques and observational records to help teachers pinpoint specific discrepancies between what they are doing and what they ought to do. At times teachers are able to diagnose these discrepancies on their own. On other occasions the skilled intervention of a supervisor is necessary. A parallel situation exists in classroom instruction. Sometimes students can self-diagnose a problem they are having in learning, and they can take remedial steps on the basis of this information. At other times students are stymied by their inability to learn a particular subject, and the teacher is needed to diagnose and remediate.

*To Help Teachers Develop Skill in Using Instructional Strategies.* If clinical supervision's only purpose were to help the teacher solve immediate problems and crises, its value would be severely limited. The supervisor would be needed each time the teacher had a "brush fire" to be put out. This is not true. The skillful supervisor uses the clinical conference and observation data to help the teacher develop enduring patterns of behavior—what we call "instructional strategies." These strategies are effective in promoting learning, motivating students, and managing the classroom. The observational techniques presented in chapters 6–9 and the criteria for effective teaching in chapter 2 deal with instructional strategies most educators believe effective. Teachers can practice these strategies and can receive objective data on improvement resulting from practice.

*To Evaluate Teachers for Promotion, Tenure, or Other Decisions.* This is the most controversial function of clinical supervision. Some supervisors avoid evaluation, but most supervisors are required by the school district or college of education to evaluate the teacher's competence, usually at the end of the supervisory cycle. Although clinical supervision emphasizes the teacher's professional development, the objective data collected through systematic classroom observation provide one basis for evaluating the teacher's competence. As we discuss later in the chapter, the "sting" of evaluation can be lessened if, as part of the clinical supervision process, the supervisor shares with the teacher the criteria and standards to be used in the evaluation report.

*To Help Teachers Develop a Positive Attitude about Continuous Professional Development.* A major goal of clinical supervision is to help the teacher realize that training does not end with the completion of certification requirements. Teachers need to view themselves as professionals, which means, in part, that they engage in self-development and skill training as a career-long effort. The clinical supervisor can model this aspect of professionalism through a willingness to develop new supervisory skills.

## Other Types of Teacher Supervision

The purpose of *clinical* supervision can be further clarified by comparing it with other kinds of teacher supervision.

*Counseling.* Many teachers—especially student teachers and first-year teachers—have overt anxiety and insecurity about their ability to perform in the classroom. Also teachers may experience temporary crises in their personal lives that interfere with classroom performance. Some teachers may suffer from chronic emotional problems (e.g., depression or unprovoked outbursts of anger) that disrupt their teaching effectiveness.

Sensitive supervisors respond to teachers' anxiety and insecurity by providing emotional support and reassurance. They also may make an effort to deal with more serious problems or may refer a teacher to appropriate specialists. In carrying out these functions, the supervisor is performing the role of counselor. Clinical supervision may also incorporate these functions, but its focus is on the teacher's instructional performance rather than the teacher's personal problems.

Another problem that arises in teacher supervision centers on career decisions. Student teachers often wonder whether they are cut out to be teachers. They may ask for assistance in seeking a teaching position or for advice about additional education. Experienced teachers may feel undecided about whether to remain in the teaching profession, to seek a transfer to another school, or to teach a different content area and grade level. The supervisor who advises a teacher about such problems is performing a counseling function rather than a clinical supervision function.

*Curriculum Support.*   Teachers sometimes ask their supervisors for advice about curriculum materials they are using. Are the materials suitable? How should they be used? Are alternative materials available? A teacher may have other curriculum concerns as well: the amount of time to spend on each curriculum topic, procedures for organizing a course of study, or new curriculum policy and guidelines in the school district.

Supervision in the form of curriculum support can be very helpful to the teacher, but it should not be equated with clinical supervision. Clinical supervision focuses directly on *actual observable events of teaching*. In contrast, curriculum support focuses on materials, objectives, and philosophy of instruction. These are major influences on teaching, but they are not the teaching act itself.

*A Note of Caution.*   Counseling and curriculum support are important, legitimate functions of teacher supervision. Teachers do experience emotional problems and curriculum concerns that may impede their instructional effectiveness. Nevertheless, a teacher may use these problems and concerns as an excuse to avoid dealing with difficulties in the act of teaching.

For example, a teacher may feel uncomfortable about the fact that students in class are generally unruly. Yet, the teacher does not wish to confront this problem and does not want the supervisor to notice what is happening. Thus the teacher steers the supervisory conference in the direction of problems and events that exist outside the classroom. (We know of instances where teacher and supervisor used their time together to talk about the problems of other teachers in the school.) When these situations occur, the clinical supervisor should listen sensitively to the teacher's comments but then tactfully steer the conference back to the teacher's own classroom behavior.

## Teacher Evaluation and Clinical Supervision

Supervisors face a conflict caused by being caught between two roles—evaluator and facilitator. Supervisors often ask, "How can I help teachers grow as persons and as classroom instructors when they know that, eventually, I must make a written evaluation of their effectiveness?" So great is the conflict that some educators have argued for a separation in roles as we shall see in Unit 5. Thus, some supervisors would evaluate teachers' performance in a manner similar to the traditional "inspector" role. Other supervisors would devote themselves to promoting teachers' development.

Teachers feel the conflict, too. They do not know whether to rely on the supervisor for support or avoid the supervisor for fear of being criticized.

This book is strongly oriented toward the role of clinical supervisor as facilitator, but we acknowledge that most supervisors must also evaluate teachers. Preservice teachers are usually evaluated at the end of their student-teaching experience by the university supervisor and cooperating teachers. These evaluations are put in placement files or reflected in written recommendations and influence their chances of obtaining teaching positions. Evaluation reports of inservice teachers may influence salary increases, promotions, and tenure decisions.

We have no easy solution for the problem created by the supervisor's dual role of facilitator and evaluator. But the following observation may help you and the teachers you supervise work toward your own resolution of the problem.

The conflict between facilitation and evaluation is not unique to teacher supervision; supervisors in all occupations and professions face the same problem. Even teachers must play the dual role at evaluator and facilitator. Teachers are charged with the responsibility of helping their students learn, but they also are required to evaluate how well students have learned relative one to another.[9]

Remember that the "sting" of evaluation can be lessened by a skillful supervisor. Teachers are most threatened when they are unaware of the criteria by which they will be judged and when they do not trust the evaluator's ability to be fair. These concerns can be alleviated by involving the teacher in the evaluative process—for example, by sharing the evaluative criteria beforehand and by basing the evaluation on objective observational data shared with the teacher. This process of sharing ideally results in teacher and supervisor working together rather than at cross-purposes.

The experience of our colleagues in the teaching profession and our own experience indicate that the vast majority of teachers are effective and can improve with supervision and training. Less effective teachers usually self-select out of the profession either duirng the preservice phase or during the first few years in the field. The realization that probability is working for them (i.e., they are more likely to be evaluated positively than negatively) helps many teachers accept the evaluative function of supervision.

Finally, we remind you of the old truism that people often learn more from their failures than from their successes. Even a negative evaluation may provide a growth experience. Supervisor and teacher may find that a negative evaluation of the teacher's performance is painful for both of them, especially if it results in the teacher's leaving the profession. One can only hope that the teacher views this leave-taking as a positive process that frees him or her to explore another profession and be successful in it.

We have more to say about the roles of clinical supervision in teacher evaluation in chapter 3. The techniques presented there can be used to promote teacher growth in addition to their application to evaluation. Planning and feedback conferences can be used to identify and share evaluative criteria. Classroom observation data can be used not only as feedback to the teacher but also as the basis for objective evaluation of the teacher's performance. This approach to teacher evaluation is discussed in more detail elsewhere.[10] The way that planning conferences, observation, and feedback fit into a state-mandated teacher evaluation process is illustrated in figure 3.1.

## The Need for Clinical Supervision

Is it necessary to make clinical supervision available to teachers? This question is worth asking, especially because research findings raise doubts about the value of this kind of supervision.

The need for clinical supervision can be defended by considering another question, "Do students need teachers?" Most educators would answer in the affirmative. All students need a teacher's

assistance at one time or another; some students need more assistance than others. Very few students are so independent that they
can learn solely by studying curriculum materials.

Teachers are in a similar situation. They, too, are learners. The
content they need to learn is the profession of teaching. At various
points in their professional development they need the skillful
assistance of a clinical supervisor if they are to make progress.

In many instances the interventions of a clinical supervisor have
made a significant impact on a teacher's growth. We recall a preservice teacher no one thought would survive student teaching. Continuous supervision of her classroom peformance and con-
sultation with school personnel helped her overcome feelings of
insecurity and learn appropriate role behaviors.

Clinical supervision can also make a difference for an inservice
teacher. We recall a teacher who was on probationary status because
of low ratings on teaching effectiveness. A sympathetic supervisor
helped the teacher through this difficult period, with the result that
he eventually was taken off probationary status. It would have been
almost impossible for that teacher to pull himself up by his own
bootstraps. The supervisor's intervention was critical.

A less serious case involved an experienced primary grade teacher
who had difficulty after accepting an invitation to teach a class of
sixth graders. The supervisor assigned to help her quickly discovered that the teacher was trying to teach the sixth-grade class in
the same manner that she had taught her second-grade classes. The
supervisor collected observational data that helped the teacher see
that her lesson plans and verbal behaviors were too simple for her
new instructional situation. With the supervisor's assistance, the
teacher was able to adjust her teaching style so that both she and the
class felt more satisfied.

## The Clinical Supervisor

Any educator responsible for the professional development of
teachers can use the techniques of clinical supervision: methods
instructors, practicum supervisors, student teaching supervisors,
cooperating teachers,[11] and school administrators to varying degrees
guide the development of preservice teachers. All these educators
can make use of clinical supervision techniques.

It has been estimated that as many as a quarter of a million
persons in the United States provide inservice education to teachers

on a full-time or part-time basis.[12] These educators include 80,000 education professors, supervisors, and consultants; 100,000 principals and vice principals; and perhaps 50,000 support personnel such as reading instructors, media experts, and mental health specialists. Each of these professionals, at one time or another, may hold conferences with individual teachers or visit their classrooms for the purpose of making observations. Anyone who interacts with teachers in these contexts may find it necessary or useful to employ the techniques of clinical supervision.

Are clinical techniques useful to those whose primary or only responsibility is the evaluation of teachers? The answer is, "Yes under certain conditions." If the evaluator intends to use classroom observation data as a basis for the evaluation, the observation techniques in chapters 6–9 will be useful. If the evaluator wishes to involve the teacher in determining the criteria for evaluation, the conference techniques in chapters 4 and 5 will facilitate this process.

We may seem to be promoting clinical supervision as a panacea to be used by all supervisors with all teachers. To a certain extent this is true. As you become familiar with the techniques of clinical supervision, you will find that they deal with basic processes—speaking, listening, influencing, observing—that occur in any supervisory contact. Because clinical supervision is built around these processes, it has a certain universality. Not all supervisors will use the "full" model of clinical supervision, however, and some will do so only under certain conditions. Other supervisors, perhaps those who see their primary role as counselor or curriculum specialist, will use only a few techniques from the clinical supervision model.

## How Effective Is Clinical Supervision?

Educators ask three important questions about the effectiveness of clinical supervision:

1. Do teachers and supervisors have a positive attitude toward the clinical supervision model? Do they like it? Is it what they want?
2. Does clinical supervision result in improved teaching in the classroom?
3. Does clinical supervision result in improved learning by the teacher's students?

This section briefly considers the research relating to each question.

*need for more/better research*

The discussion is necessarily brief because relatively little research has been done on teacher supervision. The available research has been characterized by Richard Weller as "unsystematic, unrelated to other research, globally evaluative, and of very limited scope."[13]

### Attitudes toward Clinical Supervision

Arthur Blumberg and Edmund Amidon studied the reactions of a large group of inservice teachers to supervisory conferences with their principals.[14] Specifically, they were interested in how teachers perceived supervisors' use of "direct" behaviors (e.g., giving of information, directions or commands, and criticism) and "indirect" behaviors (e.g., accepting feelings and ideas, praise and encouragement, and asking questions). The researchers attempted to relate these perceptions of direct and indirect supervisory behavior to the same teachers' ratings of conference effectiveness.

*(indirect behaviors) better received*

Blumberg and Amidon found that supervisors who emphasized indirect behaviors tended to receive high ratings from teachers on the productivity of their conferences. Teachers valued indirect supervisory conferences. As indirect communication is a major element in clinical supervision, we infer that teachers would be favorable to this model of supervision (see techniques of indirect communication in chapter 11).

James Shinn's research study asked a large sample of inservice teachers to rate the ideal frequency with which they would like school principals to use various techniques of clinical supervision and the actual frequency of such use (see figure 1.2).[15] The most significant finding is that teachers believe all the techniques of clinical supervision are worthwhile; each technique was rated as meriting occasional or frequent use. The data also confirm Blumberg and Amidon's findings: several of the highest-rated techniques (e.g., 29, 30, 31) are indirect supervisory behaviors.

A study by Gary Martin provides further evidence of teachers' acceptance of the clinical supervision model.[16] Martin surveyed a group of inservice teachers and supervisors trained in the systematic observation techniques (see chapters 6–9). A comparison group of teachers and supervisors had not received this training. Martin found that the trained teachers believed that their annual evaluation was more helpful to them than did the untrained teachers. Also, the trained teachers were more likely to accept evaluation as a basis for promotion and tenure decisions than were the untrained teachers.

Although Martin's study focused on teacher evaluation, the findings suggest that teachers also would have a positive attitude toward the observation component of clinical supervision.

How well do supervisors like clinical supervision? Two studies in Saudi Arabia (which, until recent years, used an inspector model of supervision) asked supervisors what supervisory techniques *are* being used and *should* be used (in the future or ideally). (See figure 1.2)[17,18] Another study (in Oregon) asked evaluators (administrators) to report what techniques they used before and after a new state law mandated goal setting, observation, and other aspects of clinical supervision and brief training was provided by the school district.[19] In our experience and in the experience of colleagues conducting workshops on clinical supervision, the workshops have been well received by thousands of school principals, teacher educators, and others who have participated in them. Several studies shed some light on what supervisors say they do; how well they like it varies from district to district.[20]

### *Effects of Clinical Supervision on Teaching*

Does clinical supervision help teachers improve their performance in the classroom? Norman Boyan and Willis Copeland developed an extensive training program for supervisors based on the clinical supervision model.[21] They found that supervisors trained in the model were able to help teachers make significant improvements in a variety of teaching behaviors.

In a study cited earlier, Blumberg and Amidon related teacher perceptions of supervisors' direct and indirect behaviors in conferences to teacher perceptions of learning outcomes.[22] The researchers made an interesting discovery: teachers felt they learned most about themselves, as teachers and as individuals, from conferences high in indirect *and* direct supervision.

Indirect support for clinical supervision's effectiveness can be found in the research literature on microteaching, which is a widely used set of techniques for training teachers.[23] Microteaching techniques parallel key techniques in clinical supervision. For example, in microteaching the teacher seeks to improve specific, operationally defined teaching skills; in clinical supervision the supervisor helps the teacher translate general teaching concerns into specific, observable behaviors (technique 2). Another key ingredient of microteaching is that the teacher presents a lesson in which he or she

practices several teaching skills. This lesson is recorded on audiotape or videotape, then played back so that the teacher can
receive feedback on the teaching performance. The practice and
feedback techniques of microteaching are paralleled by the classroom observation (techniques 8–21) and feedback phases (techniques 22–25) of clinical supervision. Many research studies have
demonstrated that microteaching is effective in helping teachers
improve specific teaching skills. It seems reasonable to infer that if
the clinical supervisor uses techniques parallel to microteaching,
similar improvements in teaching performance will be obtained.

### Effects of Clinical Supervision on Students

Ultimately, clinical supervision should improve student learning.
The clinical supervisor believes that if he or she can improve teacher
performance, the teacher in turn will be able to improve student
performance. If clinical supervision is effective, we should be able to
observe its effects in the supervised teacher's students. Improvements
in student attitude, classroom behavior, and scholastic achievement
represent the range of possible student effects.

Unfortunately, we have not been able to locate any convincing
research on student effects associated with clinical supervision
although our studies and those of our students clearly point in the
direction of a positive relationship.[24] A possible reason for the
lack of research is the time span required to observe effects. Such
research would require a group of supervisors who would use
the clinical supervision model with a group of teachers. After
supervision had occurred for a period of time, the researcher would
look for possible improvements in teacher performance. After
more time had elapsed, the researcher would look for possible
improvements in student performance. The research would be
costly, but it is methodologically feasible.

Indirect evidence suggests that good clinical supervision results
ultimately in improved student performance. Chapter 2 presents
teaching techniques researchers have found to be associated with
student learning. For example, students of teachers who emphasize
teaching behaviors such as praise and encouragement tend to learn
more than students of teachers who emphasize criticism and
punishment. If clinical supervision focuses on these techniques, and
if teachers show improvement in their use, then we have reason to
expect that students, too, will benefit.

In summary, the links between clinical supervision and teacher performance, and between clinical supervision and student performance, have not been convincingly demonstrated. Although indirect evidence suggests that these linkages exist, research directly focused on the clinical supervision process should be encouraged.

# Notes

1. Kimball Wiles, *Supervision for Better Schools*, 3d ed. (Englewood Cliffs, NJ: Prentice-Hall, 1967).
2. Morris L. Cogan, *Supervision at the Harvard-Newton Summer School* (Cambridge, MA: Harvard Graduate School of Education, 1961).
3. Arthur Blumberg, *Supervisors and Teachers: A Private Cold War* (Berkeley, CA: McCutchan, 1974).
4. Their work is described in several books: Robert Goldhammer, *Clinical Supervision* (New York: Holt, Rinehart and Winston, 1969); Ralph L. Mosher and David E. Purpel, *Supervision: The Reluctant Profession* (Boston: Houghton Mifflin, 1972); Morris L. Cogan, *Clinical Supervision*, (Boston: Houghton Mifflin, 1973).
5. Goldhammer, *Clinical Supervision*, p. 54.
6. Carl R. Rogers, *Client-Centered Therapy* (Boston: Houghton Mifflin, 1951).
7. Richard H. Weller, *Verbal Communication in Instructional Supervision* (New York: Teachers College Press, 1971).
8. Adapted from ibid., pp. 19–20. The list has been rephrased and items pertaining to group clinical supervision have been omitted.
9. A poignant description of the conflicts caused by the teacher's dual role is presented in Susan Edgerton, "Teacher in Role Conflict: The Hidden Dilemma," *Phi Delta Kappan* 59 (1977): 120–22.
10. Keith A. Acheson, *Techniques in the Evaluation of Teachers* (Salem: Confederation of Oregon School Administrators, 1982).
11. By *cooperating teacher* we mean a classroom teacher who supervises a preservice intern or practice teacher.
12. Bruce R. Joyce et al., *Inservice Teacher Education Report 1 Issues to Face* (Palo Alto: Stanford Center for Research and Development in Teaching, 1967).
13. Weller, *Verbal Communication*, p. 20.
14. Arthur Blumberg and Edmund Amidon, "Teacher Perceptions of Supervisor-Teacher Interaction," *Administrators Notebook* 14 (1965): 1–8.
15. James L. Shinn, "Teacher Perceptions of Ideal and Actual Supervisory Procedures Used by California Elementary Principals: The Effects of Supervisory Training Programs Sponsored by the Association of California School Administrators" (Ph.D. diss., University of Oregon, 1976).
16. Gary S. Martin, "Teacher and Administrator Attitudes toward

Evaluation and Systematic Classroom Observation" (Ph.D. diss., University of Oregon, 1975).

17. Saad Adwani, "The Relationship between Teacher and Supervisor as Perceived by Teachers, Supervisors and Principals in Secondary Schools in Saudi Arabia" (Ph.D. diss., University of Oregon, 1981).

18. Saleh Al-Tuwaijri, "The Relationship between Ideal and Actual Supervisory Practice as Perceived by Supervisors in Saudi Arabia," (Ph.D. diss., University of Oregon, 1985).

19. Keith A. Acheson, Assessment of Teacher Evaluation Process 1980–81 School Year (Cottage Grove, OR: South Lane School District).

20. Acheson, *Techniques in the Evaluation of Teachers*; Richard Darst, "Why ORS 342.850: An Analysis of Current Supervisory Evaluation Practices in Oregon Secondary Schools" (Ph.D. Diss., University of Oregon, 1982); Carolyn Ruck, "Cold War Revisited: The Use of Performance Goals in the Teacher Evaluation Process in Oregon" (Ed.D. Diss., University of Oregon, 1984); William Sears, "The Effects of an Inservice Training Program in a Model of Clinical Supervision and Persuasive Data Collection Techniques as Perceived by Teachers and Administrators: A Pilot Study" (Ph.D. Diss., University of Oregon, 1983); KiOk Yoon, "Effects of Training in Clinical Supervision on Supervising Teachers in Korean Middle Schools" (Ph.D. Diss., University of Oregon, 1983); Norman Graybeal, "Characteristics of Contemporary Classroom Supervisory Process" (Ph.D. Diss., University of Oregon, 1984); David Townsend, "The First Year of Implementation of a New Policy of Teacher Supervision and Evaluation in Five Secondary Schools of Lethbridge School District No. 51" (Ph.D. Diss., University of Oregon, 1984); Saadeh Kahlil, "The Relationship between Teacher Perceptions of Ideal and Actual Supervisory Behavior and Teacher Satisfaction with Supervision in Jordan" (Ph.D. Diss., University of Oregon, 1983).

21. Norman J. Boyan and Willis D. Copeland, "A Training Program for Supervisors: Anatomy of an Educational Development," *Journal of Educational Research* 68 (1974): 100–116.

22. Blumberg and Amidon, "Teacher Perceptions."

23. The research literature on microteaching and related techniques has been summarized by several reviewers: W. R. Borg, M. L. Kelly, P. Langer, and M. Gall, *The Minicourse: A Microteaching Approach to Teacher Education* (Beverly Hills, CA: Macmillan Educational Services, 1970); Robert F. Peck and James A. Tucker, "Research on Teacher Education," in *Second Handbook of Research on Teaching*, ed. R. M. W. Travers (Chicago: Rand McNally, 1973), pp. 940–78.

24. See note 20, above.

# 2

# Clinical Supervision and Effective Teaching

*reduce disch. actual - ideal)*
*ideal must be defined (goals)*

They who educate children well are more to be honored than
they who produce them.—*Aristotle*

We define *supervision* as the process of helping the teacher reduce
the discrepancy between *actual* teaching behavior and *ideal* teaching
behavior.[1] In this view of supervision it is important for teachers and
supervisors to develop a definition of what they mean by "ideal," or
effective, teaching. A good definition provides a basis for setting
supervision goals and assessing their attainment.

Some educators claim that effective teaching cannot be defined
because the criteria differ for every instructional situation and every
teacher. They add that good teaching is so complex or so creative
that it defies analysis. Some supervisors say that they cannot define
good teaching but can recognize it when they see it. We are sympathetic to these views, but our experience suggests that teachers
and supervisors can develop serviceable definitions of good teaching
to guide the supervisory process.

As a start, we suggest that you list five characteristics of a good
elementary, secondary, or college teacher.[2] Educators find this task
relatively easy to perform. Moreover, they usually agree with one
another's lists. Rarely do we find a controversial characteristic, that
is, a characteristic some educators think is representative of good
teaching and other educators think is representative of bad teaching.
Disagreement, if it occurs, usually concerns the relative importance
of characteristics.

Here is a list of characteristics of good teaching generated in a
workshop on teacher supervision. To what extent do these charac-

teristics agree with your list? Would you change the order of this list? See also the lists generated in two school districts (pp. 40–48).

## Characteristics of a Good Teacher

- Has positive relationships with students
- Deals with students' emotions
- Maintains discipline and control
- Creates a favorable environment for learning
- Recognizes and provides for individual differences
- Enjoys working with students
- Obtains students' involvement in learning
- Is creative and innovative
- Emphasizes teaching of reading skills
- Gives students a good self-image
- Engages in professional growth activities
- Knows subject matter in depth
- Is flexible
- Is consistent
- Displays fairness

In developing your list you may wish to examine characteristics that have interested teacher educators and researchers of teacher effectiveness. A review of their work is included in this chapter, which is organized around four different perspectives for observing what teachers do. Most of the discussion is centered on the first perspective (observation of teacher behavior) because this perspective is most closely associated with the goals of clinical supervision.

## Observation of Teacher Behavior

### *General Characteristics* 1) in classroom

The first perspective for identifying characteristics of effective teaching is to examine what teachers do in the classroom. General criteria identified by this approach are listed below under the names of the principal researchers who identified them.

### Observable Indicators of Effective Classroom Teaching

*Ryans's Factors*
1. Teacher is warm and understanding versus cold and aloof.

2. Teacher is organized and businesslike versus unplanned and slip-shod.
3. Teacher is stimulating and imaginative versus dull and routine.

*Flanders's Indicators of Indirect Teaching Style*
1. Teacher asks questions.
2. Teacher accepts students' feelings.
3. Teacher acknowledges students' ideas.
4. Teacher praises and encourages students.

*Rosenshine and Furst's Correlates*
1. Teacher is enthusiastic.
2. Teacher is businesslike and task-oriented.
3. Teacher is clear when presenting instructional content.
4. Teacher uses a variety of instructional materials and procedures.
5. Teacher provides opportunities for students to learn the instructional content.

The first three criteria of effective teaching are drawn from the work of David Ryans.[3] Ryans and his colleagues conducted an extensive program of observational studies to identify factors associated with effective teaching. Three main factors emerged from their work. The positive and negative poles of these factors are defined by (1) warm and understanding versus cold and aloof, (2) organized and businesslike versus unplanned and slipshod, and (3) stimulating and imaginative versus dull and routine. The word *surgent* is appropriate here. It may not be defined in your dictionary, but if *insurgence* is "to rise up against" and *resurgence* is "to rise up again" then *surgence* is "to rise up for" what and whom one is teaching. Teachers rated nearer the positive poles of each factor are considered more "effective" than teachers rated nearer the negative poles.

Another major set of research studies on teacher effectiveness is the work of Ned Flanders and his associates.[4] Flanders's studies observe two contrasting styles of teaching: direct and indirect. Direct teaching is characterized by teacher reliance on lecture, criticism, justification of authority, and giving of directions. Indirect teaching is characterized by teacher reliance on asking questions, accepting students' feelings, acknowledging students' ideas, and giving praise and encouragement.

A substantial number of studies have found that students of "indirect" teachers learn more and have better attitudes toward learning than students of "direct" teachers.[5] Flanders suggests, both necessary

though, that direct *and* indirect behaviors are necessary in good teaching. For example, teachers can promote learning by a direct teaching strategy, such as lecture-explanation, to clarify a difficult curriculum topic. Even in this situation, however, the teacher can make the lecture-explanation more indirect by asking questions occasionally to determine whether students are following the presentation.

Researchers have studied teacher characteristics other than direct and indirect teaching. The usual design of these studies is to observe various aspects of teachers' classroom behavior. Also, the students of these teachers are tested at intervals during the school year. Standardized achievement tests frequently are used for this purpose. The students' scores before and after a period of instruction (e.g., at the beginning and end of a school year) are compared to obtain a measure of "achievement gain." Finally, the data are analyzed to determine which teacher behaviors are associated with student achievement gains.

Barak Rosenshine and Norma Furst have done a useful review of these research studies.[6] They identified five teacher characteristics consistently associated with gains in student achievement. (By "associated" we mean that teachers with "more" of the particular characteristic tend to have higher-achieving students than teachers with "less" of the characteristic.) The first two characteristics are teacher enthusiasm (a part of "surgence") and businesslike orientation, characteristics also identified in Ryans's research. The third characteristic is teacher clarity. Researchers have defined clarity, or the lack of it, in various ways—for example, the amount of time the teacher uses to answer student questions requesting clarification of what the teacher said; the frequency with which students respond to a teacher's questions without the teacher needing to intersperse additional information or questions; and the avoidance of vague words (e.g., "some," "many," "of course") in the teacher's oral discourse.

The fourth Rosenshine and Furst teacher characteristic is variety in teaching. This characteristic can be observed by counting the number of different instructional materials, tests, and teaching devices used by the teacher. Another indicator is the extent to which the teacher varies the cognitive level of classroom discourse.

The fifth characteristic is the extent to which the teacher provides opportunities for students to learn the curriculum material covered by the achievement tests. In a sense, this characteristic reflects the extent to which the teacher "teaches to the test." However, we can view this characteristic as the teacher's ability and preference for classroom activities focused on the kinds of cognitive learning usually measured by achievement tests.

### Subject Matter: Specific Criteria

In recent years researchers have made a concerted effort to identify teacher behaviors that facilitate student learning in specific curriculum areas. Much of this research has focused on reading and mathematics instruction at the primary and elementary school levels.

Barak Rosenshine summarized and interpreted the major recent research on teacher behaviors related to success in reading and mathematics instruction in primary-level, low-socioeconomic-status (low-SES) classrooms.[7] These behaviors, which are listed below, form a pattern Rosenshine labels "direct instruction."

### Rosenshine's List of Teacher Behaviors Related to Effective Reading and Mathematics Instruction[8]

1. Classroom time is structured by the teacher.
2. Teacher devotes classroom time to reading and mathematics instruction by means of textbooks, academic workbooks, and verbal interaction.
3. Teacher assigns seatwork involving academic workbooks through which students work at their own pace.
4. Teacher organizes students into small groups and supervises their work.
5. Teacher directs activities without giving students choice of activities or reasons for the selection of activities.
6. Teacher asks direct questions that have only a single answer.
7. Teacher encourages students to attempt to answer questions, even when they say they don't know the answers.
8. Teacher immediately reinforces students on the accuracy of their answers.
9. Teacher asks a new question after student has given a correct answer.
10. Teacher gives the correct answer after a student has given an incorrect answer.

Direct instruction differs from the inquiry-oriented methods and open classroom approach sometimes recommended for primary school instruction. In contrast to these other methods, direct instruction calls for the teacher to structure students' time rather than let students structure their own time; to emphasize small-group work rather than independent learning; to engage in frequent drill rather than encourage student self-expression; and to give frequent, immediate feedback to students' answers. The research reviewed by Rosenshine suggests that the reading and mathematics achievement of primary-grade, low-SES students can be improved if the teacher uses this highly directive teaching pattern.

David Berliner and William Tikunoff conducted a large-scale research study in which they attempted to identify teacher behaviors that discriminated between more effective and less effective teachers in second-grade reading, second-grade mathematics, fifth-grade reading, and fifth-grade mathematics.[9] Teacher effectiveness was defined in terms of student gain on standardized achievement tests that measured the content of curriculum units constructed for each grade level and subject area.

Berliner and Tikunoff identified sixteen teacher behaviors that discriminated between more effective and less effective teachers at each grade level and subject area. These behaviors are listed below. As you can see, the list is in two parts: teacher behaviors that contribute to student learning, and teacher behaviors that detract from it. This list is surprisingly consistent with the findings of Ryans, Flanders, and Rosenshine and Furst.

### Berliner and Tikunoff's List of Teacher Behaviors Related to Effective Reading and Mathematics Instruction

*Effective Teacher Behaviors*

1. Teacher reacts constructively (overt, verbal, nonverbal) to students' feelings and attitudes.
2. Teacher actively listens to what a student is saying, reading, reciting.
3. Teacher gives a direction or a threat and follows through with it.
4. Teacher seems confident in teaching a given subject and demonstrates a grasp of it.
5. Teacher checks student's progress regularly and adjusts instruction accordingly.
6. Teacher expresses positive, pleasant, optimistic attitudes and feelings.
7. Teacher seems to perceive learning rate of students and adjusts teaching pace accordingly.

8. Teacher encourages students to take responsibility for their own classwork.
9. Teacher capitalizes instructionally on unexpected incidents that arise during class time.
10. Teacher prepares students for lesson by reviewing, outlining, explaining objectives, and summarizing.

*Ineffective Teacher Behaviors*
1. Teacher switches abruptly, for example, from instruction to classroom management.
2. Teacher berates child in front of others.
3. Teacher fills "empty" time periods with "busywork."
4. Teacher makes a statement whose consequences would be ridiculous if carried out.
5. Teacher often treats whole group as "one" in order to maintain peer control.
6. Teacher calls attention to self for no apparent instructional purpose.

**Teaching Strategies**  16) 任/ ( teacher Characteristics )

In the preceding section we discussed a variety of general teacher characteristics that can be assessed by observing teachers' classroom performance. It also is possible to observe teachers' use of more specific strategies and techniques. Discussion, lecture, inquiry, recitation, diagnostic-prescriptive teaching, behavior modification, independent learning contracts, simulations, and role-playing are examples of teaching strategies that competent teachers might be expected to have in their repertoire. Research has demonstrated the effectiveness of each of these teaching strategies in promoting certain types of learning, although the evidence is not always conclusive.[10]

Each teaching strategy can be analyzed further into a set of techniques. For example, some techniques viewed as desirable in recitations are (1) asking higher cognitive questions rather than knowledge-level questions exclusively, (2) pausing after asking a question to allow students time to think, (3) asking follow-up questions to help students improve their original response to a question, and (4) distributing participation among students evenly. Teachers can be observed and rated on their overall effectiveness in using this strategy and also on their effectiveness in using each technique.

Every major teaching strategy has several variants and specialized applications in different curriculum fields. For example, the discussion method can take different forms, depending on whether the teacher uses it to promote higher cognitive learning, clarification of issues, or problem solving. Subject-matter specialists also have adapted this method for their use. In social studies Oliver and Shaver have developed a variant of the discussion method that supports their jurisprudential model for analyzing public issues.[11] Unit III presents procedures for observing strategies and techniques frequently recommended by educators.

## Observation of the Teacher's Students

The second perspective for examining quality of teaching is to observe the teacher's students. Even without knowing anything about a teacher, a supervisor can make judgments about the quality of his or her teaching by observing the teacher's students. Observable aspects of student behavior and performance are listed below.

### Observable Indicators of Effective Teaching:
### Student Behavior and Performance

1. Students are learning the knowledge, understandings, skills, and attitudes intended by the curriculum, as measured by performance on tests.
2. Students exhibit independent behavior in learning the curriculum.
3. Students exhibit behaviors that indicate a positive attitude toward the teacher and their peers.
4. Students exhibit behaviors that indicate a positive attitude toward the curriculum and the school.
5. Students exhibit behaviors that indicate a positive attitude toward themselves as learners.
6. Students do not exhibit behavior problems in class.
7. Students seem actively engaged in learning the curriculum while class is in session.

Supervisors can examine test results to determine how well students are learning the curriculum, either over a short unit of study or over a school year. They can observe whether students exhibit behaviors that indicate a positive attitude toward varied aspects of schooling and whether students are well behaved during class activities.

Indicator 7 in the list is of particular importance. Barak Rosenshine and David Berliner, in a review of research on teaching, conclude that *academic engaged time* is an important factor in school achievement.[12] By academic engaged time, Rosenshine and Berliner mean the amount of time a student spends in reading, writing, manipulating, or other activities that engage the student in learning academically relevant material. In their review they found that amount of academic engaged time in reading and math activities was positively associated with student achievement in these subjects. In other words, the more time, the more achievement. Time spent on other activities was *negatively* associated with student achievement.

Academic engaged time seems an important factor in student learning. The at-task method (technique 11) provides a good observational measure of this factor.

## Observation of the Teacher's Planning

The third perspective for developing criteria of good teaching is the teacher's planning. It is easy to misjudge the effectiveness of a teacher's classroom behavior unless you know the teacher's intent and instructional objectives. For example, we recall a group of educators who observed a sixth-grade teacher conducting a question-and-answer session with her class. Afterward, one of the group criticized the teacher for asking too many knowledge-level questions. The teacher later met with the group and explained that the class needed the question-and-answer session to reinforce the information contained in a difficult lesson the preceding day. The teacher further explained that she intended to have another lesson in which students would be encouraged to reflect on and apply their newly acquired information. In brief, one of the educators had misjudged the teacher's classroom performance because he did not know the teacher's intent.

There are several possible indicators of quality in the teacher's planning efforts. It is possible to judge the soundness of the teacher's rationale in choosing instructional objectives, curriculum materials, and evaluation techniques. The teacher's rationale can be determined by talking with the teacher and examining the written lesson plans.

Another important aspect of the teacher's planning is use of student characteristics and ability to organize and individualize instruction. Evidence of good planning is also found in the teacher's approach to revising instructional plans, if necessary, based on the outcome of classroom performance.

In chapter 5 we emphasize again the need in supervision to determine the teacher's plans and intents (techniques 1–7). Without knowing them, the supervisor is likely to misjudge the effectiveness of the teacher's classroom behavior. In contrast, knowledge of a teacher's plans and intent enables the supervisor to help the teacher analyze how well his or her actual classroom behavior corresponded to what was planned.

## Observation of the Teacher Outside the Classroom

The teacher's performance in settings other than the classroom provides the fourth major basis for developing criteria of good teaching. These criteria include the effectiveness with which the teacher participates in school activities, cooperates with colleagues, and engages in professional growth activities. The extent to which the teacher's behavior conforms to ethical norms sometimes is considered a criterion of good teaching. Additional criteria can be listed— for example, the effectiveness of the teacher's participation in curriculum selection committees. At colleges and universities, research publication and service to the profession frequently are criteria for judging the teacher's effectiveness.

## Developing a Definition of Effective Teaching

The preceding discussion was not intended to provide a comprehensive definition of "good" teaching. You may disagree with some or all of the criteria presented. Our main purpose was to present perspectives from which you can develop your own definition of effective teaching. Another purpose was to acquaint you with the findings of recent research on teacher effectiveness.

We suggest that you, in your role as teacher supervisor, find time to create a personal definition of effective teaching. It is also important for teachers under supervision to develop a definition. Some supervisors and teachers have different, even conflicting, definitions of good teaching. Their definitions may include the same characteristics but differ in the relative importance they attribute to them. For example, some teachers and supervisors place greatest value on the teacher's ability to improve students' self-concepts. Other teachers and supervisors value most the teacher's ability to promote students' learning of the three R's. Chapter 11 discusses how these differences in perspective can interfere with effective supervision unless they are acknowledged and resolved.

## Notes

1. Some educators prefer the terms *good* or *effective* to *ideal*. We use these terms interchangeably in the text.
2. You can elaborate on this task by listing five or more characteristics of an ineffective teacher.
3. D. G. Ryans, *Characteristics of Teachers* (Washington, DC: American Council on Teachers, 1960).
4. Ned A. Flanders, *Analyzing Teaching Behavior* (Reading, MA: Addison-Wesley, 1970).
5. J. R. Campbell and C. W. Barnes, "Interaction Analysis—A Breakthrough?" *Phi Delta Kappan* 50 (1969): 587–90. But see also Barak Rosenshine, "Interaction Analysis: A Tardy Comment," *Phi Delta Kappan* 51 (1970): 445–46.
6. Barak Rosenshine and Norma F. Furst, "Research on Teacher Performance Criteria," in *Research in Teacher Education: A Symposium*, ed. B. O. Smith (Englewood Cliffs, NJ: Prentice-Hall, 1971), 37–72.
7. Barak Rosenshine, "Classroom Instruction," in *The Psychology of Teaching Methods: The Seventy-Fifth Yearbook of the National Society for the Study of Education*, ed. N. L. Gage (Chicago: University of Chicago Press, 1976), 335–71.
8. List is adapted from ibid., pp. 369–70.
9. David C. Berliner and William J. Tikunoff, "The California Beginning Teacher Evaluation Study: Overview of the Ethnographic Study," *Journal of Teacher Education*, 27 (1976): 24–30.
10. Much of this research is summarized in N. L. Gage, ed., *The Psychology of Teaching Methods*; and N. L. Gage and David C. Berliner, *Educational Psychology* (Chicago: Rand McNally, 1975).
11. This discussion model is described in Marsha Weil and Bruce Joyce, *Social Models of Teaching: Expanding Your Teaching Repertoire* (Englewood Cliffs, NJ: Prentice-Hall, 1978), pp. 109–80.
12. Barak V. Rosenshine and David C. Berliner, "Academic Engaged Time," *British Journal of Teacher Education* 4 (1978): 3–16.

# 3

# Clinical Supervision and Teacher Evaluation

*Summative vs formative eval,*
*↓ reduces trust, collegality*

Although the primary purpose of clinical supervision is to help teachers develop and improve through cooperative planning, observation, and feedback, it is often a part of a larger system that has as its purpose decisions about tenure, promotion, retention, and dismissal. Adding summative evaluation to formative or developmental procedures tends to reduce the collegiality and mutual trust that the supervisor and teacher need, but the two responsibilities of supervision and evaluation are often combined. In this chapter we describe the additional components we feel are needed to build a system of teacher evaluation that is consistent with the tenets of clinical supervision. These components are: district standards, job descriptions, goal setting, plans of assistance, formal evaluations, postevaluation conferences, and fair dismissal procedures. Figure 3.1 is a graphic representation of how these are all related.

## District Standards

The teacher needs to be aware of the criteria that will be used to evaluate performance. These include specific criteria for a given teacher in a particular situation and also general criteria or standards that are applied to all teachers in a district. These general criteria are best developed by a committee of teachers, administrators, and others, then adopted by the school board as official policy before copies are placed in the hands of all teachers.

The total number of standards needs to be kept under control. One way to accomplish this is to identify 15 to 20 general standards,

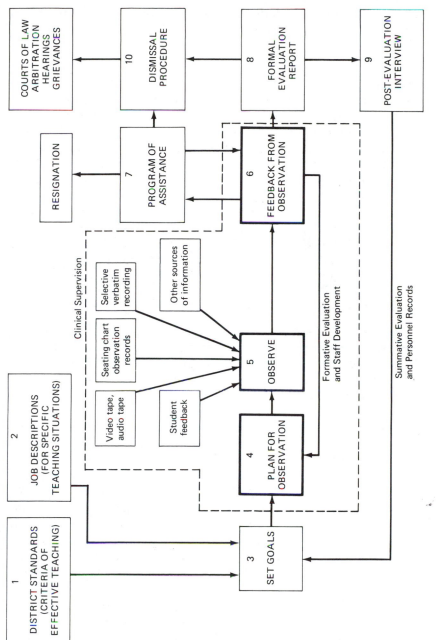

**Figure 3.1.** The teacher evaluation process. (Note that boxes 4, 5 and 6 refer to figure 1.4.) Adapted from Keith A. Acheson, *Techniques in the Evaluation of Teachers* (Salem, OR: Confederation of Oregon School Administrators, 1982).

each with three to five "indicators" stated in more explicit, behavioral terms.

### An Example

One example that was developed by this process (over a period of several years) is included on the following pages.[1] Note that the committee organized their standards around a model of what a competent teacher should do before teaching, during teaching, and after teaching. The logic of the sequence is appealing: knowing about students, setting objectives relative to that knowledge, planning instruction based on those objectives and conducting instruction that reflects the plans. Knowledge of subject matter and classroom management are components of teaching that will be important to any group of educators. Evaluation of students and communication with peers and patrons are some of the competencies that are demonstrated after teaching or outside the classroom setting.

### Another Example

Another school district took a different approach. It made use of university researchers to conduct a survey and interviews to find out what people in the community thought was a good teacher. They organized their findings in terms of the processes of teaching, products (student outcomes), and characteristics of teachers. (The results of their investigation are displayed in tables 3.1, 3.2, and 3.3.) In developing their survey questionnaire and interview questions, they also made use of the results from other research. A concurrent study asked successful coaches what they thought were important aspects of coaching. The findings are interesting, and the information gained can be used in developing or revising the standards for that particular district. It is important for each district to adopt standards that satisfy the people in that commuinity. Even though there will be substantial similarity between one community and another, there are some differences, and it is essential that the constituents have a feeling of ownership in their standards.

### Standards of Competent Performance

TEACHERS

The standards listed in this document provide the foundation for three functions of staff development. One function is to

1) Provide direction for instructional + Prof. development
2) determine Minimal standards of competent performa
3) Provide a uniform basis for eval. program

**Table 3.1.    Findings from a School District Survey of How Patrons Viewed Processes of Teaching for Importance**

| Processes | %<br>Response | Frequency | %<br>Frequency | Rank |
|---|---|---|---|---|
| 1. Treats students as persons | 45.67 | 227 | 18.8 | 1 |
| 2. Explains ideas clearly | 29.18 | 145 | 12.0 | 2 |
| 3. Asks questions causing thought | 24.74 | 123 | 10.2 | 3 |
| 4. Tells students how they are doing | 23.34 | 116 | 9.6 | 4 |
| 5. Encourages students to improve | 22.74 | 113 | 9.4 | 5 |
| 6. Encourages and uses variety of ideas | 17.10 | 85 | 7.0 | 6 |
| 7. Clearly explains why things done | 16.50 | 82 | 6.8 | 7 |
| 8. Uses variety of materials | 15.09 | 75 | 6.2 | 8 |
| 9. Accepts and uses students' ideas | 13.48 | 67 | 5.5 | 9 |
| 10. Explains where going and summarizes | 12.47 | 62 | 5.1 | 10 |
| 11. Does things several ways | 11.46 | 57 | 4.7 | 11 |
| 12. Gives students practice time | 6.84 | 34 | 2.8 | 12 |
| 13. Encourages competitiveness | 4.43 | 22 | 1.8 | 13 |
| Total | | 1208 | 100.0 | |

*Source*:   Richard L. Post et al., *The Identification and Recognition of Superior Teachers in Arlington, Washington* (Seattle: Bureau of School Service and Research, University of Washington, 1977).

*Note*:   Frequency and percentage of response for specific processes identified in the surveys listed in rank order.

provide direction for instructional and professional development. A second function is to determine if the minimal standards of competent performance for certificated teachers in the School District are met. A third function of the standards is to provide a uniform basis for the District's teacher evaluation program.

**Table 3.2.  Findings from a School District Survey of How Patrons Viewed the Products of Teaching for Importance**

| Products | % Response | Frequency | % Frequency | Rank |
|---|---|---|---|---|
| 1. Student desire to learn | 38.63 | 192 | 16.3 | 1 |
| 2. Student achievement | 29.98 | 149 | 12.7 | 2 |
| 3. Student interest in subject | 27.97 | 139 | 11.8 | 3 |
| 4. Student attitude toward school | 22.94 | 114 | 9.7 | 4 |
| 5. Student problem-solving skills | 15.69 | 78 | 6.6 | 5 |
| 6. Student attitude toward subject | 15.09 | 75 | 6.4 | 6 |
| 7. Student communication skills | 15.09 | 75 | 6.4 | 7 |
| 8. Student decision-making skills | 14.89 | 74 | 6.3 | 8 |
| 9. Student attitude toward society | 13.48 | 67 | 5.7 | 9 |
| 10. Student creativity | 12.88 | 64 | 5.4 | 10 |
| 11. Student good citizenship | 10.06 | 50 | 4.3 | 11 |
| 12. Student attitude toward adults | 8.25 | 41 | 3.5 | 12 |
| 13. Student attitude toward peers | 6.44 | 32 | 2.7 | 13 |
| 14. Student asks penetrating questions | 5.23 | 26 | 2.2 | 14 |

*Source*:   Richard L. Post et al., *The Identification and Recognition of Superior Teachers in Arlington, Washington* (Seattle: Bureau of School Service and Research, University of Washington, 1977).

*Note*:   Frequency and percentage of response for the specific products identified in the surveys listed in rank order.

A standard is composed of three parts: (1) a statement which establishes a general behavior; (2) a list of indicators which specify how that behavior will be identified; and (3) a principal's judgment as to the level of competent performance. The statement and indicators are listed for each standard. The level of

**Table 3.3.  Findings from a School District Survey of How Patrons Viewed Teacher Characteristics for Importance**

| Characteristic | % Response | Frequency | % Frequency | Rank |
|---|---|---|---|---|
| 1. Likes kids | 32.39 | 161 | 12.3 | 1 |
| 2. Enthusiastic | 25.15 | 125 | 9.5 | 2 |
| 3. Helpful to students | 22.33 | 111 | 8.4 | 3 |
| 4. Understanding and kind | 21.93 | 109 | 8.3 | 4 |
| 5. Good sense of humor | 19.99 | 99 | 7.5 | 5 |
| 6. Always prepared | 17.90 | 89 | 6.8 | 6 |
| 7. Knows subject being taught | 16.90 | 84 | 6.4 | 7 |
| 8. Friendly | 16.30 | 81 | 6.2 | 8 |
| 9. Expects much of students | 13.08 | 65 | 4.9 | 9 |
| 10. Creative | 12.88 | 64 | 4.9 | 10 |
| 11. Willing to give and take | 11.27 | 56 | 4.3 | 11 |
| 12. Sticks to business | 9.45 | 47 | 3.6 | 12 |
| 13. Listens and reacts readily | 8.65 | 43 | 3.3 | 13 |
| 14. Willing to work hard and help | 7.65 | 38 | 2.9 | 14 |
| 15. Willing to start something new | 7.24 | 36 | 2.7 | 15 |
| 16. Responsible—follows through | 5.63 | 28 | 2.1 | 16 |
| 17. Has good ideas | 4.83 | 24 | 1.8 | 17 |
| 18. Good personal appearance | 3.62 | 18 | 1.4 | 18 |
| 19. Leads well | 2.82 | 14 | 1.1 | 19 |
| 20. Works well | 2.21 | 11 | .8 | 20 |
| 21. Helpful to other teachers | 2.21 | 11 | .8 | 20 |
| Total | | 1314 | 100.0 | |

*Source*:  Richard L. Post et al., *The Identification and Recognition of Superior Teachers in Arlington, Washington* (Seattle: Bureau of School Service and Research, University of Washington, 1977).

*Note*:  Frequency and percentage of response for the specific characteristics identified in the surveys listed in rank order.

*is he/*
*she*
*trained ?*

expected performance of these standards will be determined by the professional judgment of the principal. The judgment is influenced by the teacher's assignment, class size, experience, and available resources. To determine if the requirements of the standard have been met, the statement of general teacher behavior, all of the indicators, and the performance level must be considered.

SECTION I—INSTRUCTIONAL DEVELOPMENT

*Area: Diagnosing*

Standard 1    The competent teacher establishes procedures for gathering data by:
a. completing the diagnosis for each student;
b. using the diagnostic tools which are pertinent to the teacher's goals;
c. using a variety of diagnostic instruments and techniques;
d. requesting assistance from others, when needed, for more comprehensive diagnosis.

Standard 2    The competent teacher interprets diagnostic data to identify the needs and concerns of both the individual and the group by:
a. identifying the achievement level for each student
b. explaining the significance of the achievement level diagnosed.

*Area: Prescribing - Planning*

Standard 3    The competent teacher utilizes diagnostic data to establish instructional objectives and relates these to individual needs by:
a. writing instructional objectives;
b. preparing objectives that show the data gathered in diagnosis is utilized;
c. preparing objectives in terms of student performance;
d. preparing objectives which are measurable;
e. preparing both short- and long-term objectives for any assigned class.

Standard 4    The competent teacher plans lessons to meet individual and group needs by:

a. planning lessons that are consistent with the objectives;
b. planning lessons that include appropriate activities which meet individual and group needs;
c. planning to utilize appropriate resource materials related to instructional objectives;
d. planning alternatives to meet the needs of individual students;
e. accepting and using student feedback in planning instruction.

*Area: Facilitating* — teaching

Standard 5　The competent teacher utilizes knowledge of subject matter by:
a. using words and content appropriate to the subject area and students' abilities;
b. using available media effectively and efficiently;
c. requesting and using materials and facilities based on instructional objectives;
d. knowing and utilizing community agencies, groups, and individuals to further the educational program.

Standard 6　The competent teacher uses effective classroom management techniques by:
a. showing respect for students;
b. providing an atmosphere in which students remain at task;
c. exhibiting consistency when dealing with behavior problems;
d. exhibiting positive verbal and nonverbal influence on students.

Standard 7　The competent teacher applies learning theory by:
a. utilizing and building upon students' interests and prior knowledge;
b. providing feedback as students progress toward goals;
c. allowing for a balance between intake of information and the expression of student ideas;
d. providing the individual with activities to develop attitudes, appreciations and values.

Standard 8　The competent teacher uses a variety of instruc-

tional techniques appropriate to the students'
needs by:
a. giving directions in a clear, concise manner;
b. phrasing questions so students may respond
   appropriately;
c. using strategies which involve students in
   higher levels of thinking;
d. pacing the activities within a lesson according
   to the needs of students.

*Area: Student Preformance evaluation*

Standard 9    The competent teacher establishes procedures for
              assessing student performance by:
              a. selecting means of evaluation which are
                 appropriate to the objectives;
              b. planning measurement procedures for specific
                 purposes;
              c. utilizing procedures whereby students receive
                 feedback on their individual performance;
              d. presenting information that indicates evalua-
                 tion has taken place for each student.

Standard 10   The competent teacher interprets the results of
              student performance assessment by:
              a. identifying the reasons why students have or
                 have not met the performance objectives.

Standard 11   The competent teacher utilizes the results of
              student performance assessment by:
              a. using objective data to arrive at a grade or
                 indicator of student progress to be reported to
                 parents;
              b. providing feedback that facilitates the student
                 accomplishment of goals;
              c. planning changes in teaching strategies based
                 on the results of the evaluation.

SECTION II—PROFESSIONAL DEVELOPMENT

*Area: Communication*

Standard 12   The competent teacher communicates effectively
              with students by:
              a. listening to and considering student comments
                 and suggestions;

b. being open to suggestions about ways in which to present material;

c. conveying an attitude that promotes participation in activities.

Standard 13    The competent teacher communicates effectively with colleagues and staff by:

a. participating in the group decision-making process;

b. listening to and considering suggestions from the staff;

c. sharing ideas and resources with others.

Standard 14    The competent teacher communicates responsibly to the public the significance of the school program by:

a. answering parents' inquiries promptly, honestly, and with discretion;

b. initiating when necessary communication with parents;

c. having available or locating information to relate District philosophy to the community at large.

*Area: School Relationships*

Standard 15    The competent teacher has a consistent and professional attitude toward the accomplishment of own school goals by:

a. contributing to the decision-making process and abiding by group decisions;

b. accepting shared responsibilities in and out of the classroom during the school day;

c. maintaining consistency in record keeping as defined by building or District administrative regulations and procedures;

d. using adopted courses of study or adjusting teaching objectives to include such adoptions;

e. carrying out reasonable requests given by proper authority.

Standard 16    The competent teacher has a consistent and professional attitude toward the accomplishment of District and State goals by:

a. adhering to and enforcing school law, state

> board regulations, school board policy, and
> established administrative procedures;
>
> b. adhering to the *Employee Conduct and Respon-*
> *sibility* requirements as stated in the Board
> Policy Handbook

## Another Example

Another school district (in another country) used the same questions
and format to find out what students, teachers, administrators,
board of trustee members, and parents thought was an excellent
teacher.[2] The rankings of these different groups varied—probably as
the result of their differing perspectives in respect to why the
schools exist. Criteria of teaching effectiveness may include:

- characteristics of the teacher (personality, style)
- competencies of the teacher (abilities, skills, techniques, knowledge)
- student achievement (growth in relation to ability)

District standards serve several purposes. They serve as the refer-
ence for contract renewal, promotion, and tenure decisions. They
also figure prominently in fair dismissal hearings, arbitration, and
litigation about teacher evaluation.

Over the years, our notions have changed about what the criteria
of good teaching should be. In the 1950s we looked at the characteristics of good teachers—personality variables, qualities of character,
and the like. In the 1960s attention shifted to what teachers do, or
should do, as part of the teaching process. These behaviors were
often called "competencies." Since the 1970s we have tended to talk
about "teacher effectiveness" in terms of what students are able to
do before and after working with a particular teacher.

Teacher evaluation in the past has sometimes made use of several
sources of information. Observation by supervisors is one. Another
is student ratings of teachers. Systematic observation instruments
used by others besides supervisors form another possibility. So does
self-evaluation. Gains shown by students, as measured by test
scores or other criteria, are another possible source. Scores on standardized teaching tests might be used.

Unfortunately, the most common source of information has been
the evaluator's subjective feelings, which are influenced by the

teacher's personality, style, philosophy (in relation to the evaluator's), staff relations, social patterns, and other factors which may be important but are not central to teaching effectiveness.

## Job Descriptions

Related to district standards are job descriptions. They should contain some of the same language and be consistent with the standards. In addition, they explicate the duties and responsibilities of the teacher. The district standards would be the basis for judging incompetent performance, whereas the job description would be the basis for judging neglect of duty.

Once a district has a set of standards (like the ones we have looked at) there are several possibilities for how they can be used in the process of evaluating teachers. The characteristics can be emphasized: "is neat, orderly, cooperative" or "is creative, enthusiastic, energetic." Using personal traits as the basis for summative evaluations has a long tradition but has not been very effective in either encouraging teachers to change or dismissing those who don't.

Another possibility is to use the processes as absolute standards: "reinforces positive behavior immediately and explicitly" or "does not plan lessons to meet individual needs." Beginning teachers and teachers who are insecure may welcome the reassurance of an explicit set of expectations.

A third possible use of official standards is to emphasize student outcomes: "made, on the average, a gain of one year in reading comprehension." Most teachers are apprehensive about too much emphasis being placed on what their pupils accomplish: "But you gave me a bunch of turkeys this year." As the coach of a professional football team said in turning down an attractive college job, "I don't want my career to depend on what a bunch of adolescents do on a Saturday afternoon."

A fourth possibility is to borrow an idea from business and industry and have "job targets" as an aspect of "management by objectives." To do this well one needs explicit and irrefutable descriptions of the essential elements of a particular job.

A fifth possibility—the one we advocate—is to have both a set of *standards* that apply to all teachers, and *job descriptions* that describe unique duties and responsibilities that apply to teachers with specific assignments in specialized areas of the school program. Some examples of teachers with specialized assignments are counselors, special education teachers, and resource center coordinators.

The following job description illustrates an assignment in which performance would be assessed on the basis of the primary account-abilities in addition to the general standards for all teachers.


## Position Description

POSITION: TEACHER

REPORTS TO: PRINCIPAL (OR HIS/HER DESIGNEE)

*Position Purpose:*
Implements, supervises, and maintains a high quality learning environment for students within the specific curriculum and standards of the District.

*Nature and Scope:*
The teacher is a professional with the responsibility for im-plementing a curriculum. Inherent in this responsibility is the requirement of related academic knowledge, technical skills, and professional attitudes, and judgments.

The teacher must have the ability to diagnose the needs of learners and to evaluate their performance. The teacher must also be able to prescribe learning activities appropriate to stu-dent needs and to constructively evaluate these activities. The teacher effects an optimum learning climate through appropri-ate and maximum use of all resources available and through the use of effective instructional and classroom management tech-niques.

In addition to the requirement of technical competence, the teacher maintains an attitude and conduct which is consistent with the District policy of professional conduct. The teacher follows building and District procedural guidelines and policy.

*Primary Accountabilities:*
1. Identifies the needs of students through diagnostic proce-dures and relates instructional objectives to these needs. Plans, prepares, and executes appropriate lessons, utilizing appropriate resource materials and activities.
2. Maintains student records as required by the school.
3. Communicates with parents, students, and other profession-al staff regarding student progress (behavioral and academic).

4. Follows a curriculum which is prescribed by state, District, or building.
5. Assures students of learning opportunities within a classroom environment which facilitates learning.
6. Meets the District's Standards of Competent Performance at all times.
7. Follows district and school policies, procedures, rules, regulations, and guidelines and the provisions of the contract.

The standards and job descriptions provide guidelines for teachers to refer to in setting annual goals for self-improvement, staff development, and professional advancement.

Goal can serve two kinds of needs, growth needs and deficiency needs. Teachers with deficiency needs (as identified by evaluations in respect to district standards or job descriptions) must attend to these before concentrating on goals that are strictly for personal growth. Although building on strengths is a desirable activity, it should not prevent a teacher from eliminating undesirable practices or cultivating desirable ones that have hitherto been missing.

## Performance Goals

To evaluate a teacher on the basis of the complete list of district standards would be a large undertaking if it were to be done objectively. An alternative is to concentrate on a few items that are of concern to the teacher (or to the evaluator) and agree on these as goals for a given year. The formal evaluation then is based on the progress that was made toward accomplishing the goals. If a teacher develops a serious problem in mid-year, the goals should be modified to address the problem.

Teachers have a tendency to look for "safe" goals when they know they will be evaluated on the basis of them. The evaluator needs some skill at negotiating (or insisting on) goals that are important. Skill is also required in stating goals clearly. Some questions that can be asked about a goal statement are:

- Is the called-for behavior (a) observable, (b) measurable, (c) describable?
- Is it clear what the criterion level will be? (How much is enough?)
- Under what conditions will the behavior take place?

- Is it related to the district standards or job description?
- Is it important?
- What resources will be required?
- How will the teacher proceed to reach the goal?

Figure 3.2 shows a form used in a school district to record the goals of educators (teachers, administrators, and others) for a given year.

## Formal Evaluations

Sometimes teachers are not very good at writing clear goal statements, and some administrators are not very good at writing formal evaluations. The written evaluations tend to be euphemistic and not explicit. When a dismissal occurs and the teacher has had ten years of these vague kinds of evalution, it is difficult to make the case. If one purpose for the formal evaluation is to assist the teacher's growth in instructional effectiveness, then vague generalities in the report are not very helpful. Crisply stated goals and explicit yearly evaluations could be computer-stored and accessed as a data base for making decisions about inservice staff development.

*avoid generalities*

## Plans of Assistance

"Due process" requires that before a tenured teacher is summarily dismissed for lack of competence, there will be an effort to help the teacher remedy the deficiencies. One way to do this is through an official plan of assistance. In some states this is explicitly required by law. A point of contention in dismissal hearings is often whether a plan of assistance was properly designed and carried out.

When a plan of assistance is called for, often the principal who put the teacher on notice is then expected to design and conduct the remedial program. If there is tension between the principal and the teacher (and there often is), then it is difficult to conduct a truly helpful program. We recommend the formation of a small committee to assume this responsibility. One member should be a neutral (objective) administrator; another can be a person chosen by the teacher to serve as advocate for the teacher. The third person can be someone with special knowledge, expertise, or skill in the area(s) of the teacher's deficiency.

Eugene Public Schools
School District No. 4J, Lane County
Eugene, Oregon

EDUCATOR GOAL PLAN

Educator's Name_____

Assignment _____ Year _____ Building _____

I.   GOAL STATEMENT

List the activities/behaviors you have planned to accomplish this goal.

II.  MONITORING
List the planned activities and/or procedures for measuring goal accomplishment.

Approved by _____(Supervisor's Signature) Date _____

III. ANALYZING AND ASSESSING
Educator:  Comment on the degree to which this goal was accomplished and list
the data used to support your judgment.

Educator's Signature _____ Date _____

Supervisor:  Comment on the degree to which this goal was accomplished.

Supervisor's Signature _____ Date _____

1984 – Form EG-3 (One sheet should be used for each goal developed by/for
the educator.)

**Figure 3.2.   Source: Eugene Public Schools, School District 4J, Lane County, Eugene, Oregon, 1984.**

The committee should reach agreement on what the plan of assistance will consist of, how long it will last, and what will be accepted as satisfactory evidence that the deficiency has been remedied. The committee can call on other people and resources to carry out the planned activities.

## Postevaluation Conference

The teacher and evaluator should meet to discuss the formal evaluation before it is placed in the permanent personnel file. The teacher should have the opportunity to write a rebuttal that will be filed along with the evaluation if there is irreconcilable disagreement. The postevaluation conference is also a good place to begin outlining the next year's goals for most teachers. For a few teachers this conference will be held to discuss a dismissal notice.

*relate to planning conference*

## Postdismissal Activities

When the evaluation process results in a dismissal, there are almost always additional activities. These may take many forms: grievances, arbitration, hearings, or even lawsuits. There are several implications for clinical supervision techniques in connection with these occurrences. Consider a supervisor/evaluator on the witness stand being cross-examined by the teacher's attorney.

- "On what basis were these judgments made?" (Systematic observational data recorded in the classroom, chapters 6 and through 9)
- "Did the teacher receive any feedback from these observations?" (Feedback conferences, chapter 10)
- "Was any help provided to the teacher?" (See techniques 22–25)

Several problems develop from these relationships. The use of systematic classroom observational data as evidence in a dismissal may tarnish the image of objective data as helpful to a teacher's growth. The remedial, corrective, or negative nature of a plan of assistance may diminish the luster of those same techniques that were used to promote strengths. When observation is regarded as inspection, when data become evidence, and when feedback equals criticism, the trust relationship so vital to good supervision is difficult to establish or restore. One way of dealing with this dilemma is to separate formative (growth) activities from summative (judgmental) evaluation by using colleagues for the former and evaluators for the latter.

We have studied approximately 20 dismissal cases in some depth in connection with preparing expert testimony. Several things become obvious in reading the personnel files and listening to the

*S p99, - Separate formative & summative eval,*
*colleagues          evaluators*

testimony at these hearings. If the school district administrators do a conscientious job of carrying out all the elements previously described, and if they have documented all the events carefully, they will prevail. If, on the other hand, they have been careless, arbitrary, or capricious, the teacher will win. The attorneys provided by teacher organizations are often better versed in dismissal procedures than district lawyers (who tend to be generalists).

## Conclusion

Clinical supervision is the heart of a good teacher evaluation system. The planning, observation, and feedback cycle should occur several times so that the teacher has an opportunity to grow and improve as well as to be evaluated. Where plans of assistance are required, the clinical cycle is again the key tool, but is used more frequently and with greater intensity.

School administrators tell us that when intensive assistance has been called for, approximately half of the teachers recover, a quarter resign voluntarily, and a quarter are dismissed (and usually appeal the decision). In cases where dismissed teachers have been reinstated by an arbitrator or hearing panel, it is usually because the district has failed to provide due process such as a satisfactory program of assistance. Some of the reasons for an unsatisfactory program have been:

- setting an unreasonable number of goals for the teacher
- not providing feedback after observations
- displaying evidence of prejudice or vindictiveness
- not providing sufficient time for the program to have an effect

## Notes

1. Adapted from Beaverton, Oregon, Schools Personnel Handbook.
2. *The Identification of Superior Teachers in Ft. McMurray, Alberta*, a report to the Catholic Board of Education, 1983.

# Unit Exercises

## Multiple-Choice Items

Answers are on page 214.

1. Clinical supervision includes these sequential stages:

    a. planning conference, feedback conference, classroom observation.
    b. classroom observation, feedback conference, planning conference.
    c. planning conference, classroom observation, feedback conference.
    d. counseling conference, classroom observation, feedback conference.

2. Research has shown that teachers:

    a. are satisfied with supervision as currently practiced.
    b. believe that supervision plays an important role in their professional lives.
    c. look to supervision primarily for emotional support and reassurance.
    d. hold supervision in low regard.

3. According to the authors, the major purpose of clinical supervision is:

    a. to improve the teacher's classroom instruction.
    b. to provide curriculum support to the teacher.
    c. to provide emotional support and reassurance to the teacher.
    d. (b) and (c) are correct.

4. The techniques of clinical supervision:

    a. should never be used in teacher evaluation.
    b. can be adapted for use in teacher evaluation.
    c. can be used in teacher evaluation, except for the techniques of the feedback conference.
    d. can be used in teacher evaluation, except for the techniques of the planning conference.

56

5. Which of the following generalizations is best supported by the available research evidence?

    a. Teachers prefer an indirect supervisory style.
    b. Teachers prefer a direct supervisory style.
    c. Clinical supervision results in improved learning by the teacher's students.
    d. Clinical supervision results in improved teacher retention by school districts.

6. Which of the following indicators has *not* been found to be a correlate of effective teaching?

    a. Teacher warmth
    b. Teacher enthusiasm
    c. Teacher experience
    d. Teacher clarity

7. Of the perspectives for observing what teachers do, which is the most closely associated with the goals of clinical supervision?

    a. Observation of the teacher outside the classroom
    b. Observation of the teacher's students
    c. Observation of the teacher's planning
    d. Observation of the teacher's classroom behavior

8. The behaviors of accepting students' feelings, acknowledging student ideas, and praising students are indicators of

    a. teacher task-orientation.
    b. teacher clarity.
    c. academic engaged time.
    d. indirect teaching style.

9. Which of the following elements might be an issue in a dismissal hearing?

    a. The district standards
    b. The feedback conferences
    c. The plan of assistance
    d. All of the above
    e. None of the above

10. When a supervisor is also the evaluator, what is likely to be lost?

    a. Systematic observation       c. Trust
    b. Feedback                      d. Formal evaluation

## Problems

The following problems do not have single correct answers. Possible answers are on page 215. Your answers may differ from ours yet be as good or better.

1. As a clinical supervisor, you are working with a teacher to help develop new skills while making the transition from high school teaching to junior high school teaching. One day the teacher becomes distressed and says she is considering leaving the profession. What do you do in your role as clinical supervisor?

2. You are assigned to be the clinical supervisor of an undergraduate who is just starting a student teaching placement. The undergraduate initiates a conversation with you by asking, "Are you here to evaluate me?" How should you respond?

3. Some educators claim that good teachers are born, not made. Others claim that teaching can never be analyzed because it is an art, not a science. Do you agree or disagree with these claims? Why? Why not?

# Unit II

*[handwritten: Put in outline form]*

# Techniques of Goal Setting and Planning for Observation

*[handwritten: Planning conferences; for goal setting + planning for observation]*

### Overview

There are two parts to the first stage of the clinical supervision process that require planning conferences between the supervisor and the teacher: goal setting and planning for observation. Chapter 4 considers the essentials of an effective goal-setting conference, and chapter 5 describes the elements of a conference in which the supervisor and the teacher plan for an observation. Specific techniques are described with examples of how they can be used to make conferences productive.

### Objectives

The purpose of this unit is to help you develop:

Understanding of the basic elements of a positive relationship between the supervisor and the teacher.
Specific steps for conducting a conference in which teacher and supervisor plan cooperatively to address specific concerns,

observe and record behavior, and work together to improve instruction.

Explicit techniques for providing useful feedback to teachers to aid them in analyzing, interpreting, and modifying their instructional efforts.

An approach to supervision consistent in style, strategy, and technique with the purposes set forth in unit I.

# 4

*(handwritten: put in outline form (step by step))*

# Goal Setting

*(handwritten: growth or deficiency)*
*(handwritten: teacher centered conf.)*
*(handwritten: evaluator centered conference)*

If you're not sure where you're going, you're liable to end up someplace else.—*Robert Mager*

In this chapter we look at goal setting in more detail. Practice teachers, beginning teachers, and "old pro's" all need to work toward tangible, attainable, important goals. For teachers who are working on growth goals (rather than deficiency needs) the goal-setting conference can be teacher-centered. Teachers who are on plans of assistance may need to have evaluator-centered goal-setting conferences.

Following the goal-setting conference, several cycles of planning/observation/feedback (as described in the chapters that follow) will take place. If these are conducted by the evaluator, they will result in documentation that will be used in the formal evaluation. If they are carried out by colleagues for formative purposes, it may be left to the teacher to decide whether or not data from the observations or conferences will be included in the evaluation.

## Identify the Teacher's Concerns about Instruction *(handwritten: 1)*
### (Technique 1)

The major purpose of clinical supervision is to help teachers improve their classroom instruction. One step toward this goal is to use a goal-setting conference to identify areas of instruction in which a teacher needs improvement.

A supervisor might directly ask a teacher in what ways he or she would like to improve as a teacher, but this is not usually effective. Many teachers have not formulated self-improvement goals and feel put on the spot when asked to do so. A more useful approach initially is to assist the teacher in identifying concerns. A teacher who can identify and verbalize concerns can usually take the next steps of examining the concerns objectively and solving them.

There are a variety of questions that a supervisor might ask to guide the teacher's thinking about concerns. For example: "How has your teaching been going?" "Do you find you are having more success in one area than another?" "Our goal is to help you do the best possible teaching. Are there any aspects of your teaching we should take a look at?"

No one question is better than another. The supervisor should be intent on helping the teacher reveal true concerns without feeling threatened. A threatened teacher is likely to clam up or reveal only "safe" concerns. For example, teachers have told us that "individualization of instruction" is a safe concern, but discipline is not a safe concern. A teacher who mentions discipline problems may be perceived as incompetent, whereas a teacher who mentions individualization is likely to be perceived as well along the road toward being a master teacher.

Some teachers insist that they have no concerns; their class is running beautifully. In some instances this may be an accurate perception by the teacher, but we would suggest that there is always room for improvement in one's teaching. A good teacher can get better.

When a teacher insists that he or she has no concerns, the supervisor probably should take the statement at face value. The supervisor might also suggest using a "wide-lens" observation technique such as video recording (see chapter 8), so that they can look together at the teacher's instruction. An appropriate tone can be set by asking, "How about making a videotape of one of your lessons so that we can see what aspects of your teaching please you?" After the video recording has been made and reviewed in the feedback conference, the teacher may become aware of areas for improvement that were not previously apparent.

Sometimes teachers find it helpful to examine a checklist or other instruments that will be used to evaluate their teaching performance. In showing the checklist to a teacher, the supervisor might ask, "Which of these areas do you think you're strong in? Which of these areas do you think we might take a closer look at as areas for improvement?"

Frances Fuller did a classic series of investigations at the University of Texas on teachers' concerns during training and in their professional careers.[1] She found that the concerns of preservice teachers and new inservice teachers tend to focus on the self. The concerns of experienced teachers tend to focus on their students. Fuller summarized her findings in the following form:

EARLY TEACHING PHASE: CONCERN WITH SELF

*Covert Concerns: Where do I stand?* When teaching starts, [student] teachers ask themselves, "Where do I stand?" ... "Is it going to be my class or the teacher's class?" "If I see a child misbehaving in the hall, do I handle it, ignore it, or tell someone else?" ... These concerns were rarely expressed in either written statements or in routine interviews unless directly elicited.

*Overt Concerns: How Adequate Am I?* The concern student teachers feel about class control is no secret. It is a blatant persistent concern of most beginning teachers.

Ability to control the class, however, is apparently just part of a larger concern of the new teacher with his adequacy in the classroom. This larger concern involves abilities to understand subject matter, to know the answers, to say "I don't know," to have the freedom to fail on occasion, to anticipate problems, to mobilize resources and to make changes when failures reoccur. It also involves the ability to cope with evaluation: the willingness to listen for evaluation and to parcel out the biases of evaluators.

LATE CONCERNS: CONCERN WITH PUPILS

... When concerns are "mature," i.e., characteristics of experienced superior teachers, concerns seem to focus on pupil gain and self-evaluation as opposed to personal gain and evaluation by others. The specific concerns we have observed are concerns about ability to understand pupils' capacities, to specify objectives for them, to assess their gain, to apportion out one's own contributions to pupils' difficulties and gain, and to evaluate oneself in terms of pupil gain.[2]

Frances Fuller's insights suggest the variety of teacher concerns to which the supervisor must remain sensitive. As she notes, some of these concerns are easily verbalized by the teacher. Others must be solicited through careful questioning.

## Translate the Teacher's Concerns into Observable Behaviors (Technique 2)

Helping a teacher translate concerns into observable behaviors is one of the most important techniques of clinical supervision. For an analogy, consider the patient who visits a doctor with vague complaints of not feeling well. The doctor's first task is to develop a differentiated picture of the patient's symptoms. The doctor does this by asking such questions as "How long have you felt this way?" "What are the specific problems you've been having?" "What does the discomfort feel like?" These questions are part of a diagnostic process the doctor uses, first, to isolate the problem and then to prescribe a treatment.

The clinical supervisor similarly needs to function as a diagnostician in the planning conference. Suppose a student teacher says, "I'm not sure I have the confidence to be a teacher." The teacher's expressed concern is lack of confidence, but the supervisor needs to probe further. *Confidence* may mean something different to the teacher than it means to the supervisor.

In using the technique of translating concerns, the supervisor needs to listen for the teacher's use of words and phrases that are abstract, ambiguous, or stated at a high level of generality. These typically are concepts that are one level removed from observable behavior. The following are examples of teacher statements that contain abstract or ambiguous words:

"I'm afraid I'm a *dictator*."
"To me the most important thing is for students to have a *healthy self-concept*."
"There's just not enough time to *cover everything I want to get across*."
"Some of my students are just like *wild animals*."
"I'm afraid I don't project *warmth*."
"I wonder if I'm too *critical* of students."
"How do you *reach* these *problem* students?"

When you hear a teacher use such terms to refer to a concern, your task is to clarify the terms so that they are stated in observable form. Here are examples of questions that might help the teacher state a concern more concretely:

"Do you know a teacher who projects *warmth*? What does she do?"

"What kinds of things do you do that make you think you're *critical* of students?"

"In what ways are these *problem* students?"

"Can you clarify what you mean by *reaching* problem students?"

These are not the only kinds of questions that are useful. The supervisor is free to use any questions or other technique that help the teacher focus on abstract terms and clarify their meaning.

A supervisor can judge success in translating concerns by considering this question: "Do I have enough information so that I can clearly observe the teacher's concern as it is expressed in his classroom?" Another good question is "Do the teacher and I mean the same thing when we use the term _____?" If your answer to both questions is a confident yes, this is a good indication that you are using the technique properly.

Several research studies have been done to clarify the meaning of key concepts in teaching. For example, Andrew Bush, John Kennedy, and Donald Cruikshank conducted research to determine the observable referents of teacher *clarity*.[3] Their approach was to ask students to list five behaviors performed by their clearest teacher. They were able to identify the following observable behaviors underlying the concept of clarity:

- gives examples and explains them
- repeats questions and explanations if students don't understand them
- lets students ask questions
- pronounces words distinctly
- talks only about things related to the topic he is teaching
- uses common words
- writes important things on the blackboard
- relates what he is teaching to real life
- asks questions to find out if students understand what he has told them

Although this list is not exhaustive, it is a great help to teacher and supervisor in their efforts to improve the clarity of the teacher's instruction.

Even a nonverbal concept such as teacher enthusiasm can be made observable through careful analysis. Mary Collins identified observable referents for enthusiasm by reviewing previous research on this variable, by her own analysis, and by consulting other teacher educators.[4] Collins's list of observable behaviors is presented below. Using this list as a guide, she was able to train a group of preservice elementary teachers to improve their level of enthusiasm significantly in classroom instruction.[5]

You will find more examples of observable referents for teacher concerns in chapters 6–9. These chapters present a collection of observation instruments for recording data about many different teacher concerns.

### Observable Referents for Enthusiasm

1. Vocal delivery: Great and sudden changes from rapid excited speech to a whisper; varied, lilting, uplifting intonations; many changes in tone, pitch
2. Eyes: Dancing, snapping, shining, lighting up, frequently opened wide, eyebrows raised, eye contact with total group
3. Gestures: Frequent demonstrative movements of body, head, arms, hands, and face; sweeping motions; clapping hands; head nodding rapidly
4. Movements: Large body movements; swings around, changes pace, bends body
5. Facial expression: Appears vibrant, demonstrative; changes denoting surprise, sadness, joy, thoughtfulness, awe, excitement
6. Word selection: Highly descriptive, many adjectives, great variety
7. Acceptance of ideas and feelings: Accepts ideas and feelings quickly with vigor and animation; ready to accept, praise, encourage, or clarify in a nonthreatening manner; many variations in responding to pupils
8. Overall energy: Explosive, exuberant; high degree of vitality, drive, and spirit throughout lesson

## Identify Procedures for Improving the Teacher's Instruction (Technique 3)

The first two techniques are intended to help the teacher identify concerns and translate them into observable behaviors. What happens next?

If the teacher has successfully identified some concerns, the stage is set for thinking about possible changes in instructional behavior. For example, consider a teacher who is worried that he or she comes across as dull and unenthusiastic. As the supervisor helps this teacher identify observable behaviors that comprise enthusiasm, the teacher is likely to ask. "I wonder how I could get myself to do those things." The supervisor facilitates this process by thinking aloud with the teacher about procedures that can be used to acquire new behaviors.

The simplest procedure, perhaps, is for the teacher to practice the behaviors on his own. The supervisor might say, "Why don't you make a list of these enthusiasm behaviors on a five-by-eight-inch card and keep it near you when you teach? In a week or so, I'll come in and make a video recording so you can see how you're doing."

Sometimes the needed procedures are more involved. For example, one teacher's concern may be how to use learning centers effectively. This involves a whole set of instructional skills. To acquire these skills, the teacher may need to do some reading and to attend workshops on learning centers.

If a teacher's concern is about changing student behavior, a sequence of procedures is needed. To illustrate, suppose the teacher is concerned that students do not pay attention during class discussions. The supervisor first helps the teacher to define "attention" as a set of observable behaviors—answering teacher's questions thoughtfully, looking at other students as they speak, initiating relevant comments and questions, and so forth. The teacher's next task is to develop instructional procedures that will bring about these desired "attending" behaviors. Finally, the teacher will need to practice these instructional procedures until they are mastered.

In brief, three steps are involved in bringing about change in students' behavior:

1. Identify the *specific student behaviors* you (the teacher) wish your class to use.
2. Identify the *instructional procedures* you will need to use to bring about the specific student behaviors.
3. Identify a strategy for learning and practicing the instructional procedures.

Bringing about change in student behavior is probably the most difficult goal a teacher can strive for, but it also yields the greatest rewards.

The following is an excerpt from a planning conference in which the goal was change in the behavior of second-grade children:

*Teacher:* I'd like you to come in and take a look at Randall

and Ronald. They don't do anything but play and
talk.

*Supervisor:* Are Randall and Ronald the only ones you want
me to observe?

*Teacher:* No. I have a real immature group this year. You
might as well observe all of them.

*Supervisor:* What do you mean by "immature"?

*Teacher:* Oh, they have very short attention spans, haven't
learned to settle down, and they just talk without
permission.

At this point, teacher and supervisor decided to focus on one
problem behavior—talking without permission. The dialogue continues.

*Supervisor:* Can you give an example of a situation where they
talk without permission?

*Teacher:* Well, when I have them in a small reading group,
and I ask one of them a question, any of them will
speak up if they think they have the answer.
Sometimes they don't even listen to the question,
they just say what's on their mind. And it doesn't
matter whether another child is already talking.
They'll just ignore him and speak at the same
time.

*Supervisor:* I think I have a pretty clear idea of what's happening. What do you think you can do so that only
the child you call on responds, and so that if
another child has something to say, he waits his
turn?

*Teacher:* I guess I could teach them some rules for participating. Like raising their hands when they wish to
speak and remaining quiet when another child is
speaking.

Teacher and supervisor proceeded to discuss possible methods of
teaching these rules to the children. The teacher took notes on the
procedures and agreed to practice them the following week. In

addition, the supervisor suggested that the teacher try praising or otherwise rewarding children when they obey participation rules in the reading group. In making this suggestion, the supervisor discovered that the teacher was unfamiliar with the reinforcement principles underlying the use of praise and other rewards in classroom teaching. The supervisor therefore suggested that the teacher might benefit from enrolling in an upcoming workshop on classroom management in which these principles would be discussed.

This example illustrates the three steps in bringing about change in student behavior: (1) identify the specific student behaviors desired—students raising hands when they wish to speak and being silent when another child is speaking; (2) identify instructional procedures—teaching children the instructional rules and rewarding them for appropriate behavior; and (3) identify a strategy for learning the instructional procedures—practice in the classroom and attending a workshop.

## Assist the Teacher in Setting Self-Improvement Goals (Technique 4)

If the supervisor has used the first three techniques effectively, it should be relatively easy to help the teacher take the next step: setting personal goals for improvement of instruction.

Some supervisors and teachers may feel this step is superfluous. In discussing the previous technique, we presented the example of a teacher concerned about students speaking out of turn. The supervisor helped the teacher identify several observable behaviors of students that reflected this concern and also helped the teacher identify procedures for changing these behaviors. It seems apparent that the teacher's goal is to improve students' verbal participation behaviors in reading groups. The clinical supervision process is facilitated by making this goal explicit. By doing so, teacher and supervisor both develop a clear understanding of the direction toward which the clinical supervision process is headed. It also prevents a state of confusion, with the teacher thinking, "I wonder what the supervisor expects me to be doing?"

The supervisor or the teacher can state the goal, but whoever does so should check that the other person has the same understanding of the goal and agrees with it. In the example we have been considering, the goal formulation process might occur as follows:

> *Supervisor:* To review, then, one of the things you're con-
> cerned about is students speaking out of turn.
> You've picked out a number of behaviors you'd
> like to see your students engage in. Given that, is
> there a goal you would set for yourself?
>
> *Teacher:* Yes. My first goal is to reduce the incidence of
> students' speaking out of turn. My other goal is to
> have my students engage in more positive be-
> haviors, like listening to one another and raising
> their hands when they have something to say.
>
> *Supervisor:* Those are worthwhile goals, and I'll do what I can
> to help you with them.

This interchange between teacher and supervisor, if done naturally
and genuinely, gives structure and focus to the planning conference.

## Notes

1. Frances F. Fuller, "Concerns of Teachers: A Developmental Concep-
tualization," *American Educational Research Journal* 6 (1969): 207–26.
2. Ibid., pp. 220–21.
3. Andrew J. Bush, John J. Kennedy, and Donald R. Cruikshank, "An
Empirical Investigation of Teacher Clarity," *Journal of Teacher Education* 28
(1977): 53–58.
4. Mary L. Collins, "Effects of Enthusiasm Training on Preservice Elementary Teachers," *Journal of Teacher Education* 29 (1978): 53–57.
5. Other studies agree with Collins's findings. See Edward Bettencourt,
"Effects of Training Teachers in Enthusiasm on Student Achievement
and Attitudes" (Ph.D. diss., University of Oregon, 1979); Maxwell Gil-
lett, "Effects of Teacher Enthusiasm on At-Task Behavior of Students in
Elementary Classes" (Ph.D. diss., University of Oregon, 1980).

# 5

# The Planning Conference

> The most important link between a teacher and his supervisor is effective communication.... The principal must set the stage for open communication. Teachers see the justification for supervision and evaluation programs, but they want to be a partner in the process.—*Robert L. Herchberger and James M. Young, Jr., "Teacher Perceptions of Supervision and Evaluation"*

The planning conference sets the stage for effective clinical supervision. It provides the teacher and supervisor with an opportunity to identify teacher concerns and translate them into observable behaviors. Another outcome of the planning conference is a decision about the kinds of instructional data that will be recorded during classroom observation, which is the next phase of the supervisory cycle.

*[margin handwriting: decide on type of data]*

The planning conference is organized around an agenda that calls for the identification of teacher concerns, possible solutions to these concerns, and observation techniques. Less obvious but no less important are certain processes that occur in the conference. For example, during the planning conference the teacher may decide how much trust to place in the supervisor. Trust refers to the teacher's confidence that the supervisor has the teacher's interests at heart and that the supervisor will not use data that emerge during supervision *against* the teacher. Supervisors may be technically proficient, but unless they also instill trust, their supervision is likely to be inefficient. We have more to say about trust-instilling behaviors in chapter 11.

*[margin handwriting: 1) t. cacerns 2) possible solutions 3) observation techniques]*

A basic purpose of the planning conference is to provide an opportunity for the teacher to communicate with a fellow educator about a unique classroom situation and style of teaching. Many

*[margin handwriting: Clarify style]*

*after several cycles*

teachers feel isolated in their work because they usually teach alone in a self-contained classroom. By periodically observing the teacher's classroom, the supervisor builds a set of shared experiences that supervisor and teacher can discuss together in their conferences. These conferences are especially important to the student teacher who may have no one in the school other than the supervisor with whom to share concerns and perceptions.

Planning conferences need not be long. As a supervisor, you might allow twenty to thirty minutes for the first planning conference unless the teacher has a particularly difficult problem to discuss. Later planning conferences might require only five to ten minutes, especially if there has been no change in the teacher's goals for improvement since the preceding clinical supervision cycle of planning-observation-feedback.

*neutral location*

Planning conferences probably are best held on neutral territory (e.g., the school cafeteria, if it is free) or in the teacher's classroom. Going into a supervisor's office for a conference may be perceived by the teacher as being "called on the carpet."

This chapter presents several techniques to use in the planning conference. These techniques constitute an agenda for the conference. In fact, you should consider using them in the order in which they are presented.

These techniques are important for a successful planning conference, yet we also acknowledge their limitations. A supervisor may use all these techniques and still not have a satisfactory conference because some other element (e.g., teacher's trust) is missing. There may be conference techniques that we have overlooked. Also, the techniques presented here are not highly specific prescriptions. You will need to use judgment in incorporating them into your supervisory behavior and in applying them to a particular supervisory situation. Our only claim is that judicious use of these techniques provides a sound base for conducting a planning conference. What you as a person contribute to this base is critical for success.

### Arrange a Time for Classroom Observation (Technique 5)

The first four techniques, in setting goals, involved the teacher and supervisor in *talking* about the teacher's instruction. Now it is time to plan for *observing* the instruction firsthand.

The first step in planning for observation is to arrange a mutually convenient time for the supervisor to visit the classroom. For one reason or another, there may be certain lessons the teacher does not wish you to observe or you are unable to observe because of time conflicts. The major criterion for selecting a lesson is that it should present opportunities for the teacher's concerns and solutions to those concerns. If the teacher's concern is students' responses to discussion questions, there is no point in observing a lesson in which students are engaged in independent learning projects.

Arranging a mutually convenient time for classroom observation is important for another reason. Teachers are resentful when supervisors come to their room unannounced. Teachers need to feel that the supervisor respects them as professionals and as people with first-line responsibility for their classrooms. They are not likely to feel this way if a supervisor "pops in" anytime he or she wishes to do so.

The technique of arranging a mutually convenient time is important when supervising experienced teachers, but it is equally important when working with student teachers. They can be put into a state of constant tension if they are led to think the supervisor can enter their class anytime unannounced. Arranging a time beforehand enables the student teacher to prepare instructionally (and emotionally) for the supervisor's visit. It also gives the student teacher a feeling of some control over the supervisory process. A student teacher who has this feeling of control is likely to use supervision for self-improvement rather than to feel used by it.

### Select an Observation Instrument and Behaviors to Be Recorded (Technique 6)

The planning conference is based on the teacher's *perceptions* of what occurs in the classroom. These perceptions may coincide or differ substantially from what actually occurs. Observational data are needed to provide an objective check on the teacher's perceptions and also to record instructional phenomena that may have escaped the teacher's attention. Therefore, an important step in the planning conference is for supervisor and teacher together to decide what kinds of observational data might be worth collecting.

A wise range of observation instruments is presented in unit 3. You will need to become familiar with them in order to help the teacher select an observation instrument appropriate for his or her instructional concerns.

The observation instrument should be matched carefully with the teacher's particular instructional concerns. For example, if a teacher is concerned about nonverbal behavior, a video recording (technique 15) might be appropriate. If the concern is about a problem child in the classroom, an anecdotal record (technique 14) would be helpful. Or if a teacher is concerned about the level of commotion in his classroom, a record of students' movement patterns (technique 13) could be made.

The selection of an observation instrument helps sharpen a teacher's thinking about instruction. If teacher and supervisor use the conference only to *talk* about instruction, the conversation may drift off into vague generalities and abstractions. Selecting an observation instrument brings the teacher "down to earth" by focusing attention on the observable realities of classroom instruction.

Either the supervisor or the teacher can suggest appropriate observation instruments and behaviors to be recorded on them. If the teacher is unfamiliar with methods of classroom observation, the supervisor may need to initiate suggestions. Once teachers become familiar with the range of instruments, however, they should be encouraged to initiate their own suggestions.

In discussing observation instruments with teachers, you may wish to stress their nonevaluative nature. These instruments are designed to collect nonevaluative, objective data that teachers can inspect in the feedback conference and from which they can form their own judgments about the effectiveness of their teaching. The teacher should be able to:

1. describe the lesson to be observed.
2. describe what he or she will be doing during the lesson.
3. describe expected student behaviors.
4. predict problems, "rough spots," concerns.
5. agree upon the observer's role (what will be observed and what data will be collected).

During the planning conference, the teacher-supervisor team can get the teacher to describe lesson objectives (student outcomes), to consider options among two or more teaching strategies,[1] and to plan to use specific techniques that make up the strategy. This will help to clarify what the teacher intends to do and will also give ideas on what you can plan to observe. Once the teacher states what the students are to learn from the lesson, you have a basis for deciding what instructional approaches will aid that learning and what observational methods may be appropriate.

## Clarify the Instructional Context in Which Data Will Be Recorded (Technique 7)

Throughout this book we emphasize the importance of focusing on one or two areas of concern at a time. A teacher who is asked to look at too many aspects of instruction at once is likely to become confused. Your classroom observation might focus on the teacher's enthusiasm, or discipline technique, or the task behavior of students. However, there is a risk that the recording of observational data will be oversimplified. Instructional behaviors do not occur in a vacuum. They occur in a context that must be understood if the target behaviors are to be interpreted properly.

In short, the supervisor cannot walk into a teacher's classroom "cold" and expect to understand what is happening. Therefore, an effective technique is to ask the teacher a few questions about the instructional context of the behaviors to be recorded. Since the usual instructional context is a lesson that the teacher plans to teach, you may wish to ask the teacher such questions as:

"What is the lesson that I'll be observing about?"
"What do you expect the students to learn in this lesson?"
"What strategy will you be using?"
"Is there anything I should be aware of as you teach this lesson?"

Asking these questions indicates to the teacher that you wish to understand the teacher's "world" from his or her perspective. Your presence in the classroom during the lesson will be tolerated better because the teacher and you have a shared understanding of what the lesson is about.

You need to know various observation techniques and other means of data collection in order to carry out this step. In the planning conference, both you and the teacher contribute information and ideas to figure out what you ought to look for in the observation, how you can record what happens, when you should observe, and what the two of you will do with the results.

### Constraints

It's important to be realistic about the number of contacts that you can have with a particular teacher. If your schedule limits you to two sessions per month, for example, you may not be able to include a cycle in which your observation and discussions would be needed for three consecutive days. The kinds and intervals of participation that are feasible should be understood by both the supervisor and the teacher before making plans.

### Getting Started

How do you find out what to look at? One of the ways is to use the technique we call "Translate abstract concerns into observable behaviors," if you haven't already done so in a goal-setting conference. In your early contacts with a teacher, however, you may want to limit your attention to concrete behaviors. After a few observations, both you and the teacher will be able to explore together even complex abstractions and devise observational methods for collecting pertinent information.

## Notes

1. A "strategy" is an overall approach to an instructional session. A "technique" is a specific behavior or skill that the teacher performs while implementing the "strategy." In football a pass play or a running play is strategy; blocking, running, tackling, and throwing are skills or techniques.

# Unit Exercises

Answers are on page 214.

## Multiple-Choice Items

1. General areas of agreement that should be established between teacher and supervisor are:

   *a.* teacher's goals for the year.
   *b.* mutual concerns.
   *c.* common rationale.
   *d.* teaching strategies to be considered.
   *e.* All the above are correct.

2. Goals written by teachers for their personal development and as the basis for annual evaluation may be:

   *a.* trivial
   *b.* idiosyncratic
   *c.* vague
   *d.* abstract
   *e.* all of the above

3. Which of the following assumptions about teachers are *not* compatible with the authors' view? Most teachers have:

   *a.* reasonable goals.
   *b.* access to alternative strategies.
   *c.* little need for improvement.
   *d.* preference for democratic supervision.
   *e.* adequate information and perspective on their own.

4. Which of the following topics should *not* be part of a conference to plan for an observation?

   *a.* problems or concerns
   *b.* selection of data to collect
   *c.* selection of observation instruments
   *d.* identifying what teacher and students will be doing
   *e.* suggesting solutions for the teacher's problems

5. If the supervisor is also the evaluator of the teacher,

   *a.* it will be more difficult to establish trust

    *b.* the teacher's goals may be negotiated

    *c.* the teacher is less likely to list classroom control as a goal

    *d.* the teacher is likely to be observed more frequently

    *e.* the teacher will be less defensive

6. Clarity is related to:

    *a.* questions

    *b.* vocabulary

    *c.* applications

    *d.* explanations

    *e.* all of the above

7. Abstract concepts such as warmth, enthusiasm, empathy, and altruism:

    *a.* should not be used as goals

    *b.* can be translated into observable behavior

    *c.* cannot be observed

    *d.* require a psychologist to analyze

    *e.* do not apply to teaching or supervision

8. A plan of assistance for a teacher with severe deficiencies:

    *a.* is a legal requirement in some states

    *b.* would not be supported by teacher organizations

    *c.* would forego techniques of clinical supervision

    *d.* might result in dismissal if the teacher did not improve

    *e.* should be conducted by the administrator who put the teacher on notice

## Problems

Answers are discussed on pages 215–16.

1. Think of a teacher you have known who had a severe deficiency in the techniques of teaching. Write a goal for that teacher.

2. Think of the best teacher you can remember. Write a goal for that teacher.

3. Assume you are the teacher in either problem 1 or 2 above. You are in a conference with your supervisor planning for an observation of a lesson you have prepared. What should you and the supervisor discuss?

# Unit III

# Techniques of Classroom Observation

## Overview

In order to have persuasive data available in feedback conferences, the supervisor needs a range of observation techniques and recording devices. A number of instruments and procedures are described in this unit. Most of them are easily understood and can be used effectively after a little practice. The information they provide for the teacher and the supervisor is a central element of the clinical cycle.

## Objectives

The purpose of this unit is to help you develop:

A repertoire of data-recording techniques.
Means for selecting an appropriate observation system for a given concern.
Understanding of the strengths and limitations of the various systems.
Recognition of the need for regular, systematic observation and a variety of sources of data.

# 6

# The Technique of Selective Verbatim

> Except in special instances in which some quality of timing or of sound or of sight evolved as a salient supervisory issue, written data have proven most useful and most wieldy to clinical supervisors. Perhaps the greatest advantage of a written record . . . is that Teacher and Supervisor can assimilate it most rapidly and most easily; the eye can incorporate, almost instantaneously, evidence that took a relatively long time to unfold in the lesson.—*Robert Goldhammer*

What teachers and students say to one another has a major effect on the learning process. Therefore, an important skill in teacher supervision is the ability to listen and record what is being said during classroom visitation.

*Selective verbatim* is one technique for recording events in the classroom. As the term implies, the supervisor makes a written record of exactly what is said, that is, a verbatim transcript. Not all verbal events are recorded, however. Supervisor and teacher select beforehand certain kinds of verbal events to be written down; in this sense, the verbatim record is intended to be "selective." Most of our discussion of the selective verbatim technique is concerned with identifying verbal interactions that reflect effective or ineffective teaching and thus are worth recording as part of clinical supervision.

Selective verbatim is usually done by the supervisor while the teacher's class is in progress. This is not a necessary requirement. If an audio or video recording of a class session is available (see chapter 8), a selective verbatim can be made from the recording.

As we use the term, selective verbatim implies a word-for-word

81

transcription of particular verbal statements. Suppose a supervisor is recording a teacher's questions, and the teacher asks, "What do we call animals that live exclusively off plants; you know, we have a certain name for these animals, does anyone know it?" If the supervisor writes, "What is the name of animals that live exclusively off plants?" this is not a verbatim transcription.

Selective verbatim has a number of obvious benefits and advantages as a technique of classroom observation. We mention four of them here. First, providing a teacher with a selective verbatim transcript focuses the teacher's attention on what he or she says to students or on what students say to the teacher. As a result, the teacher is sensitized to the *verbal* process in teaching. All other classroom events are screened out by the transcript.

The second advantage of selective verbatim is that it *is* selective. Teacher and supervisor do not need to respond to all aspects of the teaching-learning process, just a few simple verbal behaviors. Teachers who are trying to improve their instruction are more successful if they do not try to change many aspects of behavior at once. Changing a few behaviors at a time encourages further changes. For example, we have experienced the sense of accomplishment teachers get when they realize they are using an annoying verbal mannerism, such as "you know" or "uh," and achieve control over it. This sense of control and change motivates further, more substantial changes in teaching behavior.

A third advantage of selective verbatim is that it provides an objective, noninterpretive record of the teacher's behavior. In "live" classroom teaching, the teacher may be so caught up in the process of teaching that he or she may not hear the actual words. Even if the teacher hears, the verbal events occur rapidly and are forgotten before the teacher can reflect on their meaning and effectiveness. In contrast, selective verbatim holds a "verbal" mirror up to the teacher, which can be analyzed at the teacher's convenience.

Finally, selective verbatim has the advantage of being relatively simple to use. All that the supervisor needs is a pencil and pad of paper. Also, the verbatim transcript is made while the supervisor is in the process of observing the teacher's classroom. There is no need to do additional transcription work after the observation period.

To provide a balanced view, we should mention several potential problems that can occur with selective verbatim. A teacher who knows in advance what verbal behaviors will be recorded (e.g., the teacher's questions, verbal mannerisms, praise statements) may become self-conscious in using the behaviors. Just knowing that a supervisor will observe verbal praise, for example, may increase a teacher's use of this behavior. It is to be hoped that the teacher will gradually internalize verbal praise as a technique and use it even when the supervisor is not around.

We find in practice that teachers generally do not become self-conscious when selective verbatim is used. They are not aware of their verbal behavior and *want* to learn more about what they say and what their students say.

Another potential problem with selective verbatim arises from its "selectivity." The larger context of classroom interaction is lost if teacher and supervisor focus too narrowly on verbal behavior. A teacher may look at a selective verbatim of praise statements and dismiss them with, "Oh, I see I used verbal praise ten times. I guess that's pretty good." The analysis needs to go further to explore such questions as whether the praise was given to students who deserved it and whether it was not used when it should have been. In-depth analysis of this kind requires that the supervisor record, at least mentally, the entire flow of the lesson. A skillful supervisor is one who simplifies the teaching process by focusing the teacher's attention on a few aspects of teaching yet relates these aspects to the total context in which the behaviors occurred.

Still another problem with selective verbatim is that teacher or supervisor may select apparently trivial verbal behaviors for observation. Both supervisor and teacher need to explore why each identified verbal behavior is worth recording and analyzing. If a rationale cannot be given, they must consider whether scarce supervisory time should be used to record the particular verbal behavior.

Occasionally supervisors find that they cannot keep up with the verbal interaction. It simply occurs too fast to record. In this situation we recommend that supervisors use a symbol such as a line to indicate where they stopped recording temporarily. It is better to record a few verbal statements word for word than to paraphrase or shorten what was said.

## Teacher Questions (Technique 8)

Asking questions may well be the most important activity in which teachers engage. Aschner, for example, called the teacher a "professional question maker" and claimed that asking questions is "one of the basic ways by which the teacher stimulates student thinking and learning."[1]

Certainly teachers rely on question asking as a staple of their teaching repertoire. A half century ago, Stevens found that high school teachers asked almost four hundred questions during an average school day.[2] Unbelievable as this may seem, it is also mentioned in studies of more recent vintage. Floyd found that a sample of primary school teachers asked an average of 348 questions each during a school day.[3] In Moyer's study, elementary school teachers asked an average of 180 questions each in a science lesson.[4] In Schreiber's study, fifth-grade teachers asked an average of 64 questions each in a thirty-minute social studies lesson.[5] At the high school level, Bellack found that "the core of the teaching sequence found in the classrooms studied is a teacher's question, a pupil's response, and, more often than not, a teacher's reaction to that response."[6] These studies suggest that if a teacher and a supervisor can observe only a single aspect of classroom interaction, they might be well advised to focus on the teacher's question-asking behavior.

### Technique

The supervisor's task is to make a written record of each question asked by the teacher. Since teachers typically ask many questions, the supervisor might ask the teacher to estimate the length of the lesson. Then the supervisor uses time sampling, which means that the supervisor observes samples of the lesson (e.g., the first three minutes of the lesson, five minutes in the middle of the lesson, and three minutes at the end of the lesson). Obviously, if you are planning to observe the teacher's use of questions, you will want to select a lesson in which this verbal behavior occurs with some frequency.

It seems a simple matter to decide what is or is not a question. "How many kilometers in a mile?" is obviously a question. But how about "Johnny gave a good answer, didn't he?" or "Sue, won't you stop fidgeting in your seat?" or "I'd like somebody to tell me how many kilometers there are in a mile." The latter example is a declarative statement, not an interrogative, yet it clearly has the intent of a question.

To avoid confusion, we suggest a simple rule. If the teacher's statement is asked in a questioning manner or has the intent of a question, include it in the transcript. There is no harm in including ambiguous examples, but omitting them may cause a teacher to overlook a significant aspect of his or her question-asking behavior.

Exhibit 6.1 shows two selective verbatims based on observation of two fifth-grade teachers. The teachers assigned students to read the same brief handout on the behavior patterns and environment of the wolf, followed by a question-and-answer session to help the students review and think about what they had just read.

Teacher 1

1. Now, what do we know about this animal? What do you know about the wolf? You can refer back to this little ditto, if you'd like. Jeff?
2. Next?
3. Mike?
4. Heather?
5. Now Jeff just said that sometimes livestock . . . people or farmers hate them because they kill their livestock. Would livestock be small animals? What do you think?
6. Terry?
7. John?
8. Mike?
9. Terry, again?
10. Jeff?
11. Jerry?
12. Who said that, Jerry? Was there a quote or something in that article?
13. Do you remember the man's name?
14. Do you know something? Last night, after we read this article, after school, Jeff said, "Gee Mr. Edwards, I think I've seen that name, or something." He went right down to the library and brought back this book, and it's by the same man. Jeff, did you have a chance to look at that last night?
15. Jeff, does it just concern itself with the wolf?
16. Does anyone have anything else to say about what we already know?

Teacher 2

1. What do you know about the Arctic and that kind of area that would lead you to believe that a dog would have to be more strong there than he would have to be, say, here? Dana?
2. Pam?

**Exhibit 6.1.  Selective verbatims of fifth-grade teachers' questions**

 3. What kind of work does he have to do?
 4. Terry?
 5. Karen?
 6. Why do the dogs work harder in the north than they work here? John?
 7. Why don't our dogs have to work?
 8. What don't we need done here?
 9. Allen?
10. Doug?
11. Why do you suppose the Eskimos don't have machines? Joey?
12. Do you think so? Does anyone have another idea about why they don't, 'cause there's probably more than one idea?
13. Why would they be primitive? Pam?
14. Wanda?
15. It mentioned in the stories that wolves traveled in packs, in groups. Why do you suppose they do? What do you suppose is their reason for doing this? Joe?

**Exhibit 6.1.** (*continued*)

### Data Analysis

When teachers examine selective verbatims of their questions, they often observe the following behaviors:

*Cognitive Level of Question.*   Teachers' questions can be classified into two categories: "fact" and "higher cognitive." Fact questions require students to recall facts or information stated in the curriculum materials. Higher cognitive questions (sometimes called "thought" questions), in contrast, require students to *think* about what they have read and state their own ideas.

Fact questions and higher cognitive questions are not always easy to distinguish from one another. For example, a student may be asked to recall a fact stated in the assigned reading. The student may not be able to recall the fact but deduces it, using higher cognitive processes and other information he knows. A question that is higher cognitive in form (e.g., a "why?" question) may actually be a "fact" question if the student simply repeats an idea he heard or read elsewhere.

It is apparent that the first teacher in exhibit 6.1 is emphasizing fact questions as indicated by phrases like "What do we know?" "Who said that?" and "Did you ... look at that last night?" In contrast, the second teacher focuses on higher cognitive processes, as indicated by phrases like "What would lead you to believe?" "Why?" and "Does anyone have another idea?"

There is no convincing research evidence that one kind of question is superior to the other.[7] Their effectiveness is probably best judged by examining the teacher's intent for the lesson in which the questions occurred. If the teacher's intent is to stimulate students to think about what they have read, it seems reasonable to expect that the teacher will emphasize higher cognitive questions and use fact questions only when the student's information base is weak.

*Amount of Information.* Fact questions can be classified further into "narrow" and "broad," depending on the amount of information called for in the question. For example, the first teacher in exhibit 6.1 asked, "What do you know about the wolf?" This is an example of a *broad* fact question. "Do you remember the man's name?" is an example of a *narrow* fact question because it asks for only one bit of information. Teachers sometimes ask a series of narrow fact questions—a practice that uses up much class time and is teacher-centered—when one broad question might be sufficient.

*Redirection.* Teachers can call on one student to answer each question, or they can ask several students to respond to a particular question. That is, they can "redirect" the question. Both teachers in exhibit 6.1 used this technique, usually by simply naming the student they wished to respond. Higher cognitive questions are redirected more easily than fact questions because the former usually do not have a single correct answer. Redirection is a useful technique for increasing student participation and eliciting a variety of ideas for students to consider.

*Probing Questions.* These are "follow-up" questions designed to improve a student's initial response to a teacher question. They are not easy to detect in a selective verbatim, unless the supervisor makes special note of them (perhaps by placing a *P* beside each such question). The following is a complete verbatim of the events that transpired when the second teacher in exhibit 6.1 asked questions 6 and 7.

> *Teacher:* Why do the dogs work harder in the north than they work here? John?
>
> *John:* Well, most of the dogs here don't really have to work hard, but up north, you know, they have to do all the chores and pull sleds and everything like that.

[P] *Teacher:*  Why don't our dogs have to work?

   *John:*  They're house pets, and we do most of the work ourselves, and we don't need stuff done like they do up there.

[P] *Teacher:*  What don't we need done here?

   *John:*  We don't need dogs to pull things here. We have cars, but the Eskimos don't, so they use dogs.

The teacher's two probing questions helped John give a more complete and specific answer to the initial question.

Teachers often are unaware that they accept or overlook poor responses to their questions. A record of their probing questions provides one indication of whether this is a problem. Absence of probing questions suggests lack of attention to student responses, whereas liberal use of this technique suggests that the teacher is listening carefully to what students say and is challenging them to do their best work.

*Multiple Questions.*  The practice of asking several questions in a row can be spotted easily in a selective verbatim. Note that the first teacher begins his lesson by asking two questions in succession: "Now, what do we know about this animal? What do you know about the wolf?" The same teacher also asks multiple questions in the fifth and twelfth recorded statements. The second teacher asks multiple questions in the twelfth and fifteenth recorded statements.

Teachers usually engage in this behavior when they are "thinking on their feet." They may try various phrasings and ideas before they hit upon a question to which they wish students to respond. A teacher who asks multiple questions habitually should examine this practice to determine whether it is distracting or confusing to students. The teacher can avoid asking multiple questions by preparing questions in advance of the actual lesson.

## Teacher Feedback (Technique 9)

Research, as well as everyday observation, demonstrates that feedback has an effect on the learning process. If we are learning a new skill, we need feedback to know how correctly or well we are performing the skill. Without feedback, we may simply practice bad habits or terminate training too soon. Praise or negative remarks as a particular form of feedback also may affect our behavior, especially our motivation to learn.

John Zahorik, in his study of classroom feedback behavior of teachers, found that teachers' verbal feedback tends to be constricted.[8] Only a few kinds of feedback are used regularly. Zahorik found that the most frequent form of feedback to students was simply to repeat the student's answer to a question. Ned Flanders also found that teachers' most common form of feedback consists of simple repetition of what the pupil has said.[9] Flanders and educators in general have advocated that teachers learn how to extend the amount and variety of feedback they provide to students.

Praise and criticism as feedback are of particular interest to educational researchers. In their review of research on criticism, Rosenshine and Furst found evidence to support the generalization that "teachers who use extreme amounts or forms or criticism usually have classes which achieve less in most subject areas."[10] They also found, however, that mild forms of criticism did not produce similar results. They note that "there is no evidence to support a claim that teachers should avoid telling a student he was wrong or should avoid giving academic directions."[11]

In the same review, Rosenshine and Furst did not find a relationship between student achievement and variations in teachers' use of praise statements. Research studies not included in their review, however, especially research on behavior modification, demonstrate that teacher use of praise statements ("positive reinforcers" is the technical term) has a positive effect on student performance. The findings from this line of research also suggest that it is not helpful, in many instances, to provide negative feedback (e.g., criticism, rebukes) when students engage in socially undesirable behavior. The rule of thumb seems to be: Provide positive feedback when the student exhibits desirable behavior; avoid negative feedback when the students engage in undesirable behavior.

## Technique

As supervisor, you need to arrange with the teacher to observe a sample of classroom instruction in which there is ample opportunity for verbal interchange between teacher and students. During the classroom instruction, you record the teacher's verbal feedback statements. It also may be useful to record the immediately preceding student remark or action that prompted the feedback. Another option is to make note of the affective context: Was the verbal feedback hostile in tone? enthusiastic? automatic?

As with question classification, it is not always an easy matter to decide whether a particular teacher remark is an instance of verbal feedback. You will need to rely on your judgment to determine whether a particular remark is likely to be *perceived* by a student as feedback on his or her behavior. Thus, the supervisor needs to be a close observer of students' reactions and the total instructional context when making the selective verbatim.

Exhibit 6.2 presents a selective verbatim of a junior high school teacher's feedback statements. The lesson was organized around an article about population explosion that the students had been asked to read.

T: All right. Could someone tell me what the report was about? Ann?

S: Well, it was about birth control.

T: Birth control?

S: Uh, population explosion.

. . .

S: It was about the population explosion, but it was also about limits. It made a lot of predictions, like we won't have room to get around, and there's not going to be any room to plant crops.

T: I'm glad you remembered that the author said that these were "predictions." Why do you think I'm glad you remembered that the author used the word "predictions?"

. . .

S: I also heard that they're going to have a farm under the sea, for sea-farming.

T: Who's "they"?

S: Well . . . the scientists.

. . .

S: And as the years go by, cars will get better and better.

T: Are you sure?

S: Well, I'm not certain, but pretty sure.

T: Pretty sure. This is kind of what I wanted you to get out of this article. These are your opinions,

**Exhibit 6.2.  Selective verbatim of teacher feedback**

### Data Analysis F-back conference

The teacher and the supervisor can examine a selective verbatim of feedback behavior from several perspectives, including:

*Amount.* The simplest analysis you can make of the selective verbatim is to determine the frequency with which the teacher provides feedback. You may observe teachers who provide little or no feedback to their students. These teachers tend to use a very directive style of instruction; their primary concern is to impart knowl-

> your predictions of what might happen. And they
> sound pretty good to me, and I'll bank on them to
> a certain extent, but something might happen to
> the automobile industry so that your predictions
> wouldn't come true.
>
>     . . .

T: Who made that statement that was quoted in the article?

S: Professor Kenneth E. F. Watt.

T: Professor Kenneth E. F. Watt is saying it. Do we know that what he's saying is worthwhile?

S: Well, Professor Kenneth E. F. Watt isn't the only one that is making these predictions. There's probably thousands of people making these predictions.

T: Yes, that's a good point, Rodney. We can have some faith in what he's predicting because others are making similar predictions.

    . . .

T: Why, throughout the whole world, are there so many people having so many children? Did you ever stop to think about it? Steve?

S: When the children grow up, they want children. Then when those children grow up, then they get more children, and that goes on and on.

T: Steve, I'm not sure I'm following you. Could you clarify your idea a bit? Why do people want to have so many children?

    . . .

T: I thought the ideas you had to contribute were a lot more interesting than the article itself.

**Exhibit 6.2.** (*continued*)

edge (perhaps with too little concern about whether students are "receiving" the knowledge). Other teachers make extensive use of feedback. They tend to be more responsive to students and to encourage teacher-student interaction.

*Variety.* Of concern here is whether the teacher relies on a few limited forms of feedback (research indicates that this is what most teachers do) or whether they provide a variety of feedback. As noted, Flanders found that teachers most often provide feedback on students' ideas by acknowledging them.[12] Acknowledgment takes the form of repeating the student's idea virtually verbatim. Flanders has shown that student ideas can be acknowledged and used more effectively, for example, by doing the following:

1. *modifying* the idea by rephrasing or conceptualizing it in the teacher's own words
2. *applying* the idea by using it to reach an inference or take the next step in a logical analysis of a problem
3. *comparing* the idea with other ideas expressed earlier by the students or the teacher
4. *summarizing* what was said by an individual student or group of students

Teacher verbal feedback also can be analyzed to determine whether there is variety in the teacher's use of praise and critical or corrective remarks.

Another perspective for analyzing variety of teacher feedback is to determine the nature of the student responses that elicited the feedback statement. Does the teacher limit feedback to the information contained in the student's answer? Or does the teacher extend feedback to include the student's ideas, behavior, and feelings? Research conducted by Flanders and others indicates that teachers seldom acknowledge students' feelings, although most educators would agree that feelings—and other aspects of the affective domain—are an important part of the instructional process.

*Specificity.* Teachers tend to give simple forms of feedback, saying, "Good," "Yes, that's right," "No," or "Fine." Flanders, Zahorik, and other educators suggest that teachers should develop the habit of elaborating on their feedback by giving students an explanation for their praise or criticism. "Good, you lined up your columns of numbers very well that time" is much more specific and more helpful to a student than just saying "Good." Similarly, "I'm not sure you answered my question; listen carefully while I ask the question again" is probably more helpful than a noncommittal "Uh-huh" or "No, does anyone else have an idea?" Even a quick inspection of a selective verbatim should help a teacher see the extent to which he or she uses simple versus elaborated forms of feedback.

## Teacher Directions and Structuring Statements (Technique 10)

An important part of the teacher's role is to *manage* students' learning. Management involves giving directions and structuring the learning situation—that is, telling students what to study, how to complete an assignment or carry out an activity, what is important to remember, what to do in preparation for a test.

The findings of research support the commonsense notion that the manner in which teachers give directions to students or whether teachers give directions at all has an effect on student achievement. Rosenshine and Furst reviewed research on teachers' use of structuring statements, which can take such forms as (1) statements that provide an overview for what is to happen in a lesson; (2) summaries of what has happened in a lesson; (3) statements that indicate to a class when the teacher is switching from one topic to the next; and (4) verbal cues that emphasize the importance of some point in the lesson (e.g., "Pay particular attention to what happens next in the experiment"). Research studies consistently have found higher levels of student achievement associated with teachers who make use of structuring statements.[13]

Similar research has not been done on the effects of teacher directions, but it seems obvious that teachers who give vague, ambiguous directions will confuse students and interfere with their learning. Indirect evidence that this is true comes from research on teachers' overall clarity. Seven studies of clarity reviewed by Rosenshine and Furst found a positive relationship between the clarity of a teacher's presentation and measures of student learning.[14]

### Technique

It is probably best to observe a teacher's directions and structuring statements in the context of a complete lesson. Therefore, as supervisor, you need to speak beforehand with the teacher to determine when to begin observing and approximately how long the lesson will last. Then, during the lesson, you make a selective verbatim of each set of directions and structuring statements made by the teacher. Most of these statements occur at the beginning and the end of the lesson, so you need to be especially observant at these times.

Exhibit 6.3 presents a composite of lessons in which teachers gave directions and structuring comments. We used this approach, rather than presenting the selective verbatim of one teacher, to show the variety of forms that directions and structuring comments can take.

1. Make sure you write this down in your notebook.
2. OK. Most of you have finished. We will go on to the next poem.
3. Would someone please read the introduction?
4. Class, let's have an orderly discussion today. When you want to talk, please raise your hand and I'll call on you.
5. The report we're going to read today is about apartheid in South Africa.
6. The film we just saw on how glass is made illustrates very well some of the points that were covered in the book we're using in this course.
7. Yes, electric cars are one of the really important ways we might be able to control air pollution in the future. You might want to remember that when you write your science-fiction stories.
8. OK. Today I've shown you three different ways you can do calculations. First, we have the slide rule. Second, you can use the desk calculator. And third—does anyone remember what the third method is?
9. Let's act out this scene from the book. Who wants to be Huck Finn? Who wants to be Jim? . . . Now that we have all the characters, I want the rest of you to watch closely. See how well they do the scene as Mark Twain wrote it.
10. Now that you've finished role playing, let's talk about it. How do you feel now about Huck Finn?

**Exhibit 6.3.   Examples of teacher directions and structuring statements**

### Data Analysis

As with teacher feedback, teacher and supervisor can observe *amount*, *variety*, and *specificity* of directions and structuring comments. In addition, it is helpful to observe whether the statements are clear, that is, whether they tell the student precisely what to do.

As we stated, teacher directions and structuring comments can take a variety of forms, for example:

1. An overview of the lesson about to be presented to the class
2. The objectives and purpose of the lesson
3. Cueing remarks that focus the student's attention on key points in the lesson
4. A summary of what was covered in the lesson
5. Statements that relate the lesson to curriculum content previously covered or to events outside the classroom
6. Directions concerning what students are to do while the lesson is in progress, after the lesson is completed, or if a student completes an assignment while other students are still working
7. Reinforcement of key directions and structuring comments by repeating them in another format (e.g., through a handout, on the blackboard, or by an overhead projector)

This list is not exhaustive, but it does illustrate the range of teacher comments and actions you can include in a selective verbatim of directions and structuring comments.

### Notes

1. M. J. Aschner, "Asking Questions to Trigger Thinking," *NEA Journal* 50 (1961): 44–46.
2. R. Stevens, "The Question as a Measure of Efficiency in Instruction: A Critical Study of Classroom Practice," *Teachers College Contributions to Education*, no. 48 (1912).
3. W. D. Floyd, "An Analysis of the Oral Questioning Activity in Selected Colorado Primary Classrooms" (Ph.D. diss., Colorado State College, 1960).
4. J. R. Moyer, "An Exploratory Study of Questioning in the Instructional Processes in Selected Elementary Schools" (Ph.D. diss., Columbia University, 1966).
5. J. E. Schreiber, "Teachers' Question-Asking Techniques in Social Studies" (Ph.D. diss., University of Iowa, 1967).

6. Arno Bellack, Herbert Kliebard, Ronald Hyman, and Frank L. Smith, Jr., *The Language of the Classroom* (New York: Teachers College Press, 1966).
7. Barak Rosenshine and Norma Furst, "Research on Teacher Performance Criteria," in *Research in Teacher Education: A Symposium*, ed. B. O. Smith (Englewood Cliffs, NJ: Prentice-Hall, 1971), 37–72.
8. John A. Zahorik, "Classroom Feedback Behavior of Teachers," *Journal of Educational Research*, 62 (1968): 147–50.
9. Ned A. Flanders, *Analyzing Teaching Behavior* (Reading, MA: Addison-Wesley, 1970).
10. Rosenshine and Furst, "Teacher Performance Criteria," p. 51.
11. Ibid.
12. Flanders, *Analyzing Teaching Behavior.*
13. Rosenshine and Furst, "Teacher Performance Criteria," pp. 51–52.
14. Ibid., pp. 44–45.

# 7

# Observational Records Based on Seating Charts

*These seating chart techniques look simple, but they're not. True, all the supervisor gives you to look at is a seating chart with lines and arrows all over it. But they tell you a lot about what happened in your lesson. You can see that your teaching is following a definite pattern. Then the question you need to ask yourself is, Is this a good or a bad pattern, something I want to change or something I want to keep on doing?—Comment of a high school teacher*

Several techniques for observing teacher and student behavior make use of seating charts. This family of observation instruments is sometimes called Seating Chart Observation Records (SCORE).

One of the main advantages of SCORE instruments is that they are based on classroom seating charts. Since teachers use seating charts in their daily work, they usually find it easy to interpret SCORE data.

SCORE instruments have several other advantages. They enable the supervisor to condense a large amount of information about classroom behavior on a single sheet of paper. SCORE instruments can be created on the spot to suit the individual teacher's concerns. They are easy to use and interpret. Moreover, they get at important aspects of classroom behavior, such as students' level of attentiveness and how teachers distribute their time among students in the class. A special benefit of SCORE instruments is that they enable teacher and supervisor to spotlight individual students in the class, at the same time observing what the class as a whole is doing.

SCORE instruments do have several limitations and disadvan-

tages. They simplify the teaching process by isolating certain behaviors for observation, but unless these behaviors are related to the
total teaching-learning context, the teacher may draw simplistic conclusions from the data. Another hazard is that teacher or supervisor
may select trivial behaviors for observation. As a supervisor, you
should also be aware that sometimes classroom behavior will "speed
up" or become chaotic. In this situation, you may need to modify or
temporarily abandon the data-collection process.

## At Task (Technique 11)

The at-task technique was developed in the 1960s by Frank Mac-
Graw at Stanford University.[1] MacGraw devised a system of classroom observation that used a 35 mm camera, remotely controlled.
From the front corner of the room the camera took a picture of the
total class every 90 seconds, using a wide-angle lens. The photos
were developed and enlarged. The observer was then provided with
a set of pictures of a classroom during a given time period (e.g., 20
pictures to represent a 30-minute lesson).

A variety of results were obtained. Some looked like the films
formerly shown in nickelodeons, where the students gradually
move from a position of sitting erect at their desks to a position of
sleeping with their heads on their desks, back to a position of sitting
and looking attentive. Other collections of pictures showed students
working feverishly on matters that had nothing to do with the task
at hand, or vacant from their seats talking to their neighbors, or
engaged in a variety of actions the teacher regarded as inappropriate.

The data obtained from the pictures were valuable for the teacher
in understanding individual students. But the method of collecting
data was so demanding, expensive, and time-consuming that experiments were conducted using alternative methods. Ultimately a
paper-and-pencil technique was developed to provide much the
same data as the 35 mm camera. This paper-and-pencil technique
has come to be known as "at task." A completed "at task" is shown
in Exhibits 7.1 and 7.2.

Research studies have demonstrated that student at-task behavior
is an important factor in learning. This finding has intuitive appeal.
It seems obvious that the more a student attends to the tasks presented by the teacher, the more he or she will learn. The correlation
between at-task behavior and learning is not perfect, however. One

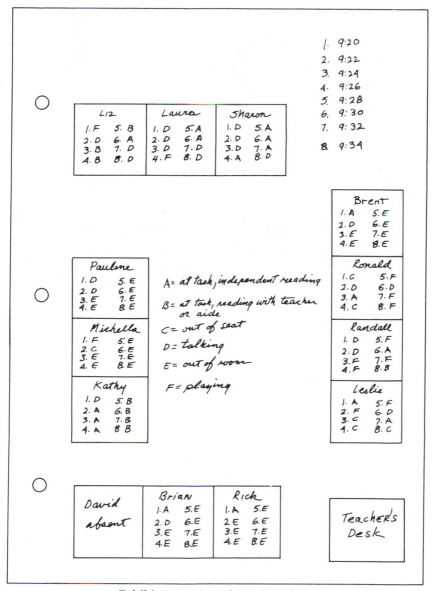

**Exhibit 7.1. At-task seating chart**

student may attend carefully to a teacher's lecture or to the words in a textbook, yet end up confused and unable to master the lesson content. Another student may work eagerly on the assigned task but may fail to learn because he or she is using incorrect or inappropriate behaviors; for example, using "regrouping" incorrectly in computation problems. Nonetheless, if students are at task, one can conclude with some confidence that learning is taking place.

Because there is a clear link between student at-task behavior and learning, the at-task observational technique is probably the most important of the SCORE procedures.

### Technique

The intent of at-task observation is to provide data on whether individual students during a classroom activity were engaged in the task or tasks that the teacher indicated were appropriate. Before an observer can use this technique, then, he must be acquainted with what the teacher expects the students to be doing during a given classroom period. In other words, the teacher rather than the supervisor defines what constitutes at-task behavior.

Typical at-task behaviors are reading, listening, answering questions, drawing a map, and working cooperatively to complete a group project. Those classrooms where one task is expected of all students usually present no problem, but where students are able to do a variety of tasks, some preparation is necessary before the supervisor can use this technique. If the variety of tasks is too complex, teacher and supervisor may choose to limit the observation to one group or section of the classroom.

To use the at-task technique the supervisor must complete these seven steps:

1. Stations himself in a section of the room where he is able to observe all students.
2. Constructs a chart that resembles a seating pattern of the students in the room that day.
3. Indicates on the chart the sex and some other identifying characteristic of each student. The latter is necessary when the students are not known to the supervisor.
4. Creates a legend to represent at-task behavior and each type of inappropriate behavior observed. A typical legend might be
   A: At task
   B: Stalling
   C: Other schoolwork than that requested by the teacher
   D: Out of seat
   E: Talking to neighbors

5. Systematically examines the behavior of each student for a few seconds in order to determine whether the student is at task, that is, doing what the teacher considers appropriate. If so, indicates this by marking a 1A in the box on the seating chart meant to represent the student. Exhibit 7.1 indicates that this is the first observation; the letter A refers to at-task behavior. If the student is not at task, the observer indicates this by recording 1B, 1C, 1D, or 1E (using the legend created in step 4).

6. Repeats step 5 at three- or four-minute intervals for the duration of the lesson using the same letter legend to indicate observed behavior but changing the number to indicate the sequence of observations. For example, 3A in a box indicates that the student was at task during the supervisor's third observation.

7. Indicates time of each set of observations. This is marked somewhere on the chart (e.g., see upper right-hand corner of exhibit 7.1).

You are advised to follow a few precautions in using the at-task technique. First, avoid forming too many categories for observation. Step 4 (above) listed five categories—at task, stalling, other schoolwork than that requested by the teacher, out of seat, and talking to neighbors—which is probably as many categories as you would want to form. Adding more categories complicates observation greatly, and it becomes increasingly difficult for the teacher to interpret the resulting data. In many classroom observations two categories are sufficient: at task and off task.

In using the at-task technique, supervisors sometimes become overly concerned about the accuracy of their observations. It helps to realize that observation of at-task behavior requires a moderate degree of inference. The expression on a child's face may be interpreted as thoughtful reflection about what the teacher is saying or as daydreaming. We suggest you think "probabilistically." If you think it is more probable that the child is engaged in thoughtful reflection than in daydreaming, use the at-task category. If you think it is more probable that the child is daydreaming, indicate this by using one of your off-task codes. You may wish to tell the teacher that the completed chart is, to an extent, subjective. Thus the teacher should look for general patterns rather than question the accuracy of a few isolated observations.

The at-task chart in exhibit 7.1 has one box for each student in the class. The students are identified by name on the chart. If the feedback conference occurs fairly soon after the observation, the teacher should have no difficulty matching students with the boxes even without names. However, if the feedback conference is delayed, you should consider putting students' names in the appropriate boxes of the seating chart. This creates a problem if the teacher does not have a prepared seating chart to assist you and if you don't know the students' names. A simple solution is for the teacher to have students say their names aloud at the beginning of the class period while you jot them down; the student's first or last name should be sufficient.

You may wish to use several different colored pencils or pens to record at-task data. The seating chart can be one color, and the at-task observations can be a different color. This procedure results in a visually pleasing product for the teacher to study and interpret.

### Example

An elementary school principal observed a first-grade teacher's reading class. The decision to do an at-task seating chart grew out of a planning conference between the teacher and the principal. Part of this conference is reproduced below:

T:  Would you come in and do an at task in my classroom? Randall and Ronald do nothing but play and talk. I would like to see just how much they really work.

P:  Are Randall and Ronald the only ones you want me to observe?

T:  No. I have a real immature group this year. You might as well observe all of them.

P:  What do you mean by "immature"?

T:  Oh, they have very short attention spans, haven't learned to settle down, and they are all talking without permission. In other words, this first grade doesn't really know how to settle down and do some work.

P:  Do they seem to understand what you have planned for them?

T:  Yes, but they have a hard time settling down to work. Ronald moans and groans most of the time or plays.

*P:*   What kinds of behavior should I observe for the at task? What categories should I use?

*T:*   Before I forget, remember some of my children are out of the room for music at the time you're coming.

*P:*   That's right. I'll put it on my checklist so I won't forget it.

*T:*   Check to see if they're out of their seats, talking, playing, or at task. They will also be reading to my aide or to me.

*P:*   I'll make note of the reading aide, and I'll see you tomorrow.

For the purpose of this observation, at-task behavior was defined as independent reading in a workbook at one's seat (*A*) or as reading with the teacher or aide (*B*). The principal also recorded several other categories of behavior: out of seat (*C*); talking (*D*); out of room (*E*); playing (*F*). The categories are shown in the legend in exhibit 7.1, together with the completed at-task seating chart. Exhibit 7.2 presents a data summary of children's at-task behavior.

### Data Analysis

Exhibit 7.2 provides a convenient summary of the observations recorded on the seating chart (exhibit 7.1). The teacher can see at a glance how many children were engaged in each category of

| BEHAVIOR | 9:20 | 9.22 | 9:24 | 9:26 | 9:28 | 9:30 | 9:32 | 9:34 | Total | % |
|---|---|---|---|---|---|---|---|---|---|---|
| A. At task independent work | 4 | 1 | 2 | 2 | 2 | 4 | 2 | 0 | 17 | 18% |
| B. At task reading with teacher or aide | 0 | 0 | 1 | 1 | 2 | 1 | 1 | 2 | 8 | 8% |
| C. Out of seat | 1 | 1 | 1 | 2 | 0 | 0 | 0 | 1 | 6 | 6% |
| D. Talking | 5 | 8 | 2 | 0 | 0 | 2 | 2 | 3 | 22 | 23% |
| E. Out of room | 0 | 1 | 5 | 5 | 5 | 5 | 5 | 5 | 31 | 32% |
| F. Playing | 2 | 1 | 1 | 2 | 3 | 0 | 2 | 1 | 12 | 13% |

**Exhibit 7.2.   Summary of at-task data from Exhibit 7.1.**

behavior—either at a particular point in time or summed across all the time samples.

Analysis of at-task data is illustrated nicely by the feedback conference that occurred between the principal and the first-grade teacher. Part of this conference is reproduced below:

T:   Let's see. Randall was at task once. Ronald was, too. Here is a shocker! Liz, Laura, and Sharon do a lot of visiting. I can see where I need to do some changes in the seating.

P:   That may solve some of your talking and visiting problems.

T:   Boy, from nine-twenty to nine-thirty-six five of my students are out to music. This only leaves seven to work with. Gee, I only worked with two children, and the aide worked with one.

P:   It seems as though quite a few of your students are gone at one time.

T:   Yes, I should try to work with these students before they go to music.

P:   That's a good idea! In that way you can usually have them read to you every day.

T:   Maybe I could ask the aide to have Kathy only read a few pages and then listen to someone else.

P:   That sounds great!

T:   This doesn't solve my problem with Randall and Ronald. Since Brian and Rick go to music, maybe I could put Ronald at Rick's desk. This way I can get a direct view of him. This also would separate the two boys.

P:   This sounds like a good step. Maybe you'll want to keep the boys apart permanently in the classroom.

T:   I sure hope this works. If not, I'll find something else.

P:   I'm sure you will. You seem to have some good ideas already.

T:   I could even have the aide work with Ronald and Randall in reading and have her play some phonics games with them. This would help expand their attention span, too.

*P:* You're really getting some good ideas. It will be interesting to see how they work out. Maybe I could come back and do an at task again.

*T:* Yes, I'd like to see if some of my ideas will help the children settle down, especially Ronald and Randall.

This interaction between principal and teacher illustrates the importance of at-task data in clinical supervision. The data focus the teacher's attention directly on the extent to which students are engaged in productive classroom behavior. If students are not at task, the teacher knows that there is a problem that needs correction. As in the example, teacher and supervisor can develop solutions once the problem has been diagnosed.

In inspecting exhibits 7.1 and 7.2, you might note the rapid change in behavior characteristic of young children. Except for those who left the room, the children were likely to change from one category of behavior to another with each observation. For example, Leslie varied back and forth between behavior categories *A, C, D,* and *F* within the 14-minute (9:20 to 9:34) period of observation.

## Verbal Flow (Technique 12)

Verbal flow is primarily a technique for recording who is talking to whom. It also is useful for recording categories of verbal interaction—for example, teacher question, student answer, teacher praise, student question. Verbal flow is similar to the technique of selective verbatim (see chapter 6) in that both techniques deal with classroom verbal behavior. Selective verbatim is concerned more with the actual content of the verbal communication, whereas verbal flow identifies the initiators and recipients of the verbal communication and the kind of communication in which they are engaged.

A study by Gregg Jackson and Cecilia Cosca highlights the importance of recording verbal flow data.[2] Their study was sponsored by the U.S. Commission on Civil Rights to determine whether teachers in the Southwest distributed their verbal behavior differently among Anglo and Chicano students.[3] Observers recorded verbal behaviors in fourth-, eighth-, tenth-, and twelfth-grade classes in 52 schools. A modified form of the Flanders Interaction Analysis System (see chapter 9) was used to classify each verbal interaction and whether it was directed to, or initiated by, an Anglo student or a Chicano student.

Jackson and Cosca found that teachers directed significantly more of their verbal behaviors toward Anglo students than toward Chicano pupils. The most striking results were that "teacher praised or encouraged Anglos 35% more than they did Chicanos, accepted or used Anglo's ideas 40% more than they did those of Chicanos, and directed 21% more questions to Anglos than to Chicanos."[4] The researchers also found that Anglo students initiated more verbal behaviors than did Chicano students. It may be argued that the differences in teacher verbal behaviors reflect the fact that Anglo students in these classrooms were generally higher academic achievers than the Chicano students. Even if true, this means that teachers probably should be directing *more*, not fewer, verbal behaviors to Chicano students.

Research has identified other forms of bias in teacher verbal behaviors. Dunkin and Biddle reached the following conclusions in their review of one of these research studies:

> the majority of both *emitters* and *targets* [of verbal behavior]—whether they be teachers or pupils—are located front and center in the classroom. Thus, pupils who are located around the periphery of the classroom are more likely to be spectators than actors in the classroom drama. It could be, then, that if the teacher wants to encourage participation on the part of a quiet pupil or silence on the part of someone who is noisy, she need merely move the pupil to another location in the room![5]

Although teachers tend to talk more to students seated closest to them, other "location" biases can occur. For example, one teacher found that he had a tendency to acknowledge more questions from students seated to his right than from students seated to his left. After learning of this tendency, the teacher realized that, in talking to a class, he usually looked to the right side of the classroom. Thus, students seated to this side were in the teacher's central line of vision, whereas students to the left were in his peripheral vision. It occurred to the teacher how frustrated students to his left might be if they had questions but could not ask them because they were out of his line of sight. With this new awareness, the teacher made a conscious effort to distribute eye contact equally to all parts of the classroom. This led to a more equal distribution of verbal behaviors.

Research on discussion groups has identified a number of factors related to differences between students in verbal behavior. In a review of this research Meredith and Joyce Gall found that black students tend to participate less in discussions than white students, and younger students tend to participate less than older students.[6] Also, males tend to initiate more verbal acts than do females. This sex difference has been found to occur even among young children.

Verbal flow is a valuable supervisory technique because it helps teachers discover (1) biases in their own verbal behavior, and (2) differences between students in verbal participation. Verbal flow is particularly appropriate when the lesson involves discussion, question-and-answer recitation, or other methods that require many verbal interchanges between teacher and students. It is not appropriate for observing instruction low in verbal interaction (e.g., lecture and independent study).

### *Technique*

As with other SCORE observational instruments, the first step in doing a verbal flow is to make a classroom seating chart. Because of the many seating patterns that can occur in classrooms, we suggest that you not have a standard form; rather, create the seating chart on a blank sheet of paper.

A box is used to represent each student. You can put the students' names in the appropriate boxes, or if you wish to focus on a particular characteristic, you can just indicate the characteristic. For example, the teacher may suggest in the planning conference that you label each student as male or female; characteristically verbal or non-verbal; and high-achieving, average, or low-achieving. Of course, the teacher will need to tell you the labels that apply to each child. The advantage of this kind of chart is that a teacher can more easily determine whether he or she responds differentially to students who vary in these characteristics.

Arrows are used to indicate the flow of verbal interaction. The base of the arrow indicates the person who initiates a verbal interaction, and the head of the arrow indicates the person to whom the comment is directed.

The teacher is an exception to this procedure. Because the teacher usually initiates most of the verbal interactions, it would be awkward to have an arrow leading from the box that designates the teacher to each student to whom a comment is directed. Arrows would be crisscrossing one another as they made their way from the teacher's box to boxes situated at diverse points of the seating chart.

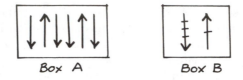

This problem is avoided by placing the arrow completely within the student's box. The base of the arrow should come from the general direction of the teacher. This means that the teacher made these statements directed toward this student.

One way to keep a verbal flow chart visually simple is to use notches in an arrow to indicate repeated interactions of the same kind. For example, in box A a separate arrow is used to record each interaction. Analysis of these data indicates that the teacher directed four comments to this student, and the student directed two comments back to the teacher. The same data are recorded in box B by two arrows. The arrow indicating the teacher-initiated comment has three notches on it. The arrow indicates one comment, and each notch represents a comment, for a total of four teacher-initiated comments. Similarly, box B indicates a total of two student-initiated comments.

The standard verbal flow chart can be elaborated by using additional categories of observation. The following are possible teacher categories:

———→ + teacher praise or encouraging remark
———→ − teacher criticism or negative remark
———→ ? teacher question
———→ | teacher asks a question or makes a comment to the class
           as a whole

Student verbal behaviors also can be differentiated, for example:

———→ √ student volunteered a relevant or correct response
———→ × student volunteered an irrelevant or incorrect response
———→ ? student question
———→ | student comment directed to the class as a whole

The teacher should participate during the planning conference in deciding what categories are to be observed. It is inadvisable to form more than a few categories. Otherwise the recording and interpretation of verbal flow data become unwieldy.

Some supervisors prefer to use an alphabetic notation system rather than arrows. Letters of the alphabet indicate discrete categories of verbal interaction; for example:

$Q$    teacher question
$P$    teacher praise
$C$    teacher criticism
$R$    student volunteered a relevant or correct response
$X$    student volunteered an irrelevant or incorrect response
$q$    student question

Teacher and student behaviors are easily distinguished by the use of upper-case and lower-case letters.

Either arrows or alphabetic notation will get the job done. The choice of one or the other is a matter of preference.

### Example

The assistant principal of a high school, one of whose responsibilities is teacher supervision, was asked by a first-year English teacher to determine which students were contributing to classroom and small-group discussions. The teacher's purpose was not to use the supervisor's data to evaluate the students but to learn whether she was influencing students' participation and how nonparticipating students could be encouraged to join the discussion.

Teacher and supervisor agreed that a verbal flow chart was an appropriate technique for collecting the data. The supervisor arranged to visit the teacher's class at a time when a discussion was scheduled.

The verbal flow chart made by the supervisor is presented in exhibit 7.3. Horizontal lines are used to indicate empty desks. Students' sex is indicated by an $M$ or $F$. The supervisor recorded verbal flow data into four categories: teacher question, student response, teacher positive response, and teacher negative response. Because some students talked among themselves, the supervisor decided to record this behavior by drawing an arrow between the students engaged in such talk. The period of observation was 22 minutes.

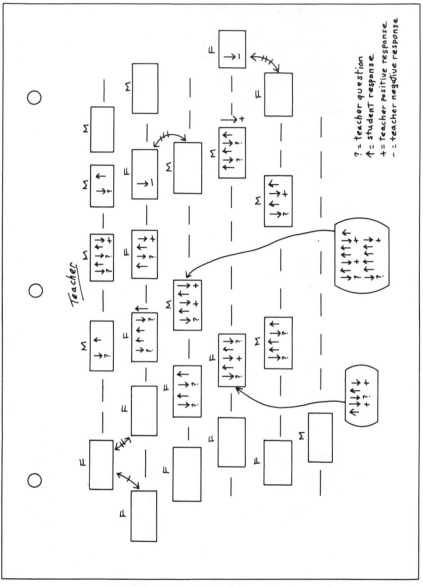

**Exhibit 7.3.   Verbal flow chart**

## Data Analysis

Verbal flow data can be analyzed from various perspectives. They include the following:

*Seat-Location Preferences.*   As we mentioned, some teachers direct more of their attention to students seated in a certain part of the room. This is quite apparent in the teacher's verbal flow chart. As she herself noted, she suffers from tunnel vision. You can see in exhibit 7.3 that she asked most of her questions of students seated directly in her line of sight. Students on either side of her line of sight were ignored. This is a common pattern even among experienced teachers. You also may have noted that comments among students, while the lesson was in progress, occurred only at the periphery of the seating arrangement.

 On seeing the verbal flow chart, the teacher commented that she might solve the problem of tunnel vision by seating students closer together, using the available empty seats. Another suggestion is to place students in a circular seating arrangement so that everyone can have eye contact with one another.

*Student Preferences.*   In exhibit 7.3 students are characterized by sex. One can ask whether the teacher interacted equally with boys and girls, and whether she used each category of verbal behavior equally with them.

The verbal flow chart indicates that 13 girls and 11 boys were present for the lesson. Of the 20 questions asked by the teacher, 12 (60 percent) were directed to boys, and 8 (40 percent) were directed to girls. Of the 12 positive responses by the teacher, 8 (66 percent) were directed to boys and 4 (33 percent) were directed to girls. The 2 negative responses by the teacher both were directed to girls. Nine of the 13 girls (70 percent) and four (36 percent) of the 11 boys did not participate in the lessons. These data suggest a sex bias favoring boys.

You might also note in exhibit 7.3 that two students, a boy and a girl, dominated the participation. (The supervisor needed to create additional boxes to contain their data.) Thirty percent of the total number of questions asked by the teacher were directed to these two students. Moreover, they accounted for nearly half the student responses.

*Verbal Behavior Preferences.*   Verbal flow charts can be inspected to determine how frequently teachers and students use certain behaviors and whether they emphasize certain behaviors more than others. One contrast of interest in exhibit 7.3 is the teacher's use of

positive response behavior compared with her use of negative response behavior. Of the teacher's fourteen responses, all but two
were positive. The two negative responses were directed toward
girls near the periphery of the classroom.

Another possible comparison in exhibit 7.3 is the number of student responses followed by a teacher positive response versus the
number of student responses not followed by a teacher positive
response. There were 32 student responses in the lesson. Of these,
12 (38 percent) were accompanied by a teacher positive response.
This is a relatively high percentage, compared with teachers' usual
practice.

## Movement Patterns (Technique 13)

Another use of seating charts is to record the movements of teacher
and students during a class lesson. We call this SCORE technique
"movement patterns." The supervisor's task is to record how the
teacher and individual students walk from one section of the room
to another during a given time interval. This focus on *movement*
differentiates movement patterns from the other SCORE techniques
presented in this chapter: at task, which focuses on students' level
of *attentiveness and engagement* in classroom tasks; and verbal flow,
which focuses on the nature and direction of *verbal communication* in
the classroom.

Many teaching situations, especially in primary and elementary
school, require teachers to make decisions about where to position
themselves in the classroom. For example, as students file into class
after recess, the teacher needs to decide whether to stand by the
door, at the desk, or elsewhere. When students are engaged in
seatwork or group projects, the teacher must decide whether to stay
at the desk or move around the room checking on students' work.

The nature of the teacher's movement patterns may affect classroom control and student attentiveness. The teacher who "hides"
behind a desk may have more discipline problems than the teacher
who checks on students as they work at their desks. The teacher
who always stands in one position while speaking to the class may
not hold students' attention as effectively as the teacher who moves
about for dramatic emphasis or to illustrate a concept on the blackboard or chart.

Teachers may also reveal a consistent bias in their movement
patterns. They may prefer one part of the classroom over another,

perhaps because certain students are seated here. Some teachers consistently stand some distance away from students' seats while speaking to the class. This may create difficulties for students who do not see or hear well, and it may provide an excuse for some students to engage in off-task behavior ("the teacher can't see what I'm doing").

Students' movement patterns may reveal whether or not they are at task. Sometimes it is necessary for students to move about the classroom to complete an assigned activity. At other times students move about to avoid an assigned task or because they have no assigned task. The latter situation often occurs when students finish their work early in the class period; they mill around to find a classmate to engage in conversation or to find another activity.

Movement patterns can be recorded during any lesson, but the technique is most useful when the teaching situation contains the potential for movement about the classroom. For example, seatwork and group projects provide situations where the teacher needs to move about, and where students *do* move about even when they don't need to. On the other hand, the showing of a film or a question-and-answer recitation places many constraints on teacher and student movement. There is not likely to be much movement behavior to record.

### Technique

The seating charts used in other SCORE instruments often consist of *interconnected* boxes, as in exhibit 7.1. To record movement patterns, each student and the teacher should be represented by *self-contained* boxes. Also, the seating chart should represent the physical layout of the classroom, including aisles and desks or tables where students might congregate.

Exhibits 7.4 and 7.5 show a seating chart used to record movement pattern data. Teacher or student movement from one point in the room to another is indicated by a continuous line. The line for each originates at the point where that person was located in the room when the supervisor began observing. The teacher and students are likely to move from one point to another, stop for a while, then move to another. Each stopping point should be represented by an indicator—for example, an arrow (————→————), a circle (————⊖————), or X (————✕————). Exhibit 7.4 uses circled numbers to indicate stopping points. This physical movement chart shows that the

Physical Movement Legend

X X X X X X  Directed student movement

– – – – – – Purposeful student movement (nondirected)

———————— Teacher movement (arrow indicates direction)

•••••••••••• Nonpurposeful student movement

①      Student–teacher conference (number indicates sequential order)

**Exhibit 7.4.   Physical movement**

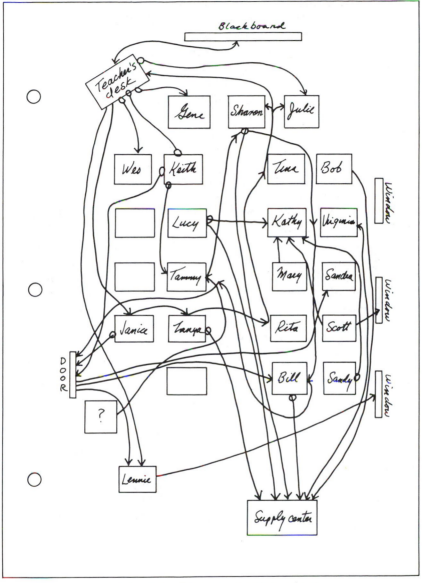

**Exhibit 7.5.  Movement pattern chart**

teacher started the lesson standing at the front of the classroom, next moved to the student designated by box 1, and then proceeded to student 13.

A single line with a different symbol at each end can be used when a person goes from his desk to another location and then returns to his desk. For example, in exhibit 7.5 the teacher went from her desk (designated by O) to Wes's desk and then returned to her desk. In contrast, Keith went from his desk to the teacher's desk and then returned.

You may wish to indicate the pattern of movement at different points in the lesson. A supply of different colored pencils is useful for this purpose. For example, you might record the first ten minutes in yellow, the second ten minutes in green, and so on. If the teacher plans to divide the lesson into different activities, this can form the basis for color coding. The first activity might be direction giving, followed by small-group projects, followed by whole-class question-and-answer. Movement during each activity can be recorded with a different colored pencil. This technique helps the teacher analyze the pattern of movement that occurred at different stages of the lesson.

Occasionally so many students will mill about in the classroom that you will not be able to record all their movements. When this occurs, you may find it necessary to suspend data recording for a few minutes. (Make a note that you did so somewhere on your movement pattern chart.) Another possibility is to limit your observation to only certain students in the classroom.

### Example

The movement pattern chart in exhibit 7.5 was recorded in a high school typing class. The teacher worried about whether he ran "too loose a ship." He didn't think that students should be "chained to their desks" during the entire class period, yet he wanted to instill in students a sense of discipline and self-control. He and the supervisor agreed that a movement pattern chart might be a good method for recording the extent of order-disorder in the classroom. The supervisor observed and recorded the class's movement behavior for approximately 30 minutes.

### Data Analysis

At first glance a movement pattern chart such as the one shown in exhibit 7.5 looks like a hopeless maze. If teacher and supervisor isolate the behavior of one person or one section of the room, however, they usually can make helpful inferences from the chart.

The first thing that caught the teacher's eye was the door leading into the classroom. Six students entered or left the classroom after the lesson had begun. One student who was not enrolled in the class (indicated by a "?") apparently entered the classroom, talked to several friends and then left. The teacher thought that the mystery student probably was wandering about during his free study period. The chart also indicates that two other students (Bill and Sandra) entered late. Two students (Janice and Keith) left the class while it was in session and then returned. The teacher did not realize this had happened.

After inspecting these data, the teacher decided he needed to monitor students' entry and exit behavior more closely. Also included in this resolution to himself was the decision to give students some ground rules about leaving class while it is in session.

The teacher then focused his attention on his own movement behavior. He recalled that he had gone to the blackboard at the start of the lesson to write down key terms relating to typing business letters. Keith then came to his desk to ask a question. Next the teacher decided to check on students' progress, so he visited a few students (Lennie, Wes, Gene, and Julie), each time returning to his desk to catch up on some paperwork. Finally, he decided he should circulate a bit; this is reflected in the large loop starting and ending at his desk. Although he did not stop at every student's desk, he felt he got to each area of the classroom so that if a student desired to speak with him, the student could get his attention easily. The teacher generally felt satisfied with his movement pattern in this lesson.

He and the supervisor next turned their attention to the supply center. Six students (Tanya, Lucy, Sharon, Bill, Virginia, and Bob) went to the center for supplies during the observed part of the lesson. After seeing these data, the teacher wondered whether he should ask students to get any necessary materials at the start of the lesson. This procedure might create a more orderly class and might help students become more organized and systematic in their approach to typing. The supervisor suggested that the teacher experiment with this procedure and see for himself whether it produced the desired effects.

Finally, the teacher looked at other student behavior. He noted that several students had visited with each other, and in fact four of them (Lucy, Mary, Scott, and Sandy) had congregated around Kathy's desk. Two students (Scott and Lennie) had gone to the window to see what was happening outside. The supervisor told the teacher that most of this kind of classroom movement occurred near the end of the observation period. The teacher realized then that he had an activity planned for students who finished early but had forgotten to relay it to them because he was preoccupied about some paperwork he wanted to complete during the lesson.

Summing up his inferences from the movement chart data, the teacher felt that he might make a few changes that would create a more orderly class without losing the relaxed atmosphere he valued.

# Notes

1. Frank MacGraw, Jr., "The Use of 35-mm Time-Lapse Photography as a Feedback and Observation Instrument in Teacher Education" (Ann Arbor, MI: University Microfilms, No. 66–2516, 1966).
2. Gregg Jackson and Cecilia Cosca, "The Inequality of Educational Opportunity in the Southwest: An Observational Study of Ethnically Mixed Classrooms," *American Educational Research Journal* 11 (1974): 219–29.
3. The report of the Jackson and Cosca study used the term "Anglo" to refer to white persons not of Spanish-speaking background. "Chicano" was used to refer to Mexican-Americans.
4. Ibid., p. 227
5. Michael J. Dunkin and Bruce J. Biddle, *The Study of Teaching* (New York: Holt, Rinehart and Winston, 1974), p. 226.
6. Meredith D. Gall and Joyce P. Gall, "The Discussion Method," in *The Psychology of Teaching Methods*, ed. N. L. Gage (Chicago: National Society for the Study of Education, 1976).

# 8

# Wide-Lens Techniques

It was a shock to listen to the audiotape of my lesson. I never knew before how I sounded when talking to students. The idea of audiotaping lessons is good. After all, students have to hear you talk, so you might as well know how you sound to them. Just listening for a few minutes to the audiotape helped me learn quite a few things about how I communicate. I'm ready now to have myself videotaped. I want to see what that's like!—*Comment of a preservice secondary teacher*

## Anecdotal Records (Technique 14)

The advantage of structured observation instruments such as at task, selective verbatim, and movement patterns is that they enable you to focus on a few classroom behaviors. Other classroom noise is screened out. But sometimes it is the "noise" (i.e., what you didn't plan to observe) that's most interesting. A particular teacher statement may strike you as especially good or bad or noteworthy. Possibly the teacher did something that made you think, "I wonder why she did that?"

Anecdotal records are a way to record classroom interaction using a wide lens. The basic technique is to make brief notes of events as they occur in the classroom. These notes form a "protocol" of what happened. Indeed, this is a favorite technique of anthropologists, who are highly trained in the process of making notes that objectively describe what happens in a different culture. The process of making intensive, direct observations is called *ethnography*.

The process of making good anecdotal records in supervisory observations is similar to the ethnographies anthropologists make in observing the workings of different cultures. (Isn't the classroom a "culture"?) In fact, educational researchers are making increasing use of ethnographic methods to learn how classrooms function. For example, David Berliner and William Tikunoff employed ethnographers to record observations of classrooms known to vary in learning effectiveness.[1]

We use *anecdotal record* to describe this technique because it suggests informality and reminds teacher and supervisor that the record is not complete. Like any other classroom observation technique, the anecdotal record provides a selective set of data for the teacher to examine. Another reason for the label anecdotal record is that it is less esoteric than, say, ethnographic protocol, to which this technique is related.

### *Technique*

The anecdotal record is a good technique to use when the teacher cannot think of specific behaviors that should be observed. This situation is most likely to occur in the beginning stages of supervision, that is, when the teacher is first learning about the planning conference—classroom observation—feedback conference cycle. The teacher may comment, "I guess I'd just like a general idea of what I'm like as a teacher." As supervisor, you might then suggest the anecdotal record as a broad-focus technique for collecting descriptive data about teacher and student behavior. Audio and video recordings, discussed later in this chapter, are other possibilities.

The anecdotal record is a broad-focus technique, but you and the teacher will need to decide just how wide to open the lens. You can make anecdotal observations of the teacher, one student, one group of students, the whole class of students, or everyone in the class (teacher, students, teacher aides, etc.). The wider the lens, the more behaviors can be observed. As you narrow the lens, you will have a narrower set of behaviors to observe, but you will also have the opportunity to make more intensive descriptions of these behaviors.

The anecdotal record usually consists of short descriptive sentences. Each sentence summarizes a discrete observation. You may wish to start each sentence on a separate line and every so often record the time that an observation was made. Thus the teacher can get a sense of the temporal flow of the events that occurred.

The sentences should be as objective and nonevaulative as possible. Instead of writing "Students are bored," you might note "Sev-

*teacher makes Conclusions / interpr,*

eral students yawn; Jane looks out window." Instead of writing "Teacher does good job of giving directions," you might note "Teacher gives clear directions. Asks if students understand. Most of class nod or say yes." If you make evaluative comments in your anecdotal record, the teacher is likely to react to the evaluation rather than to what occurred. If your comments are descriptive and neutral, the teacher can more easily form conclusions about the effectiveness of the lesson.

Teacher and student behaviors are not the only events to observe and describe in the anecdotal record. You should be alert also to the *context* of the teacher's lesson; for example:

"The room is warm; wall thermometer reads 78 degrees."
"Teacher shows map to class. Map is faded. Names of countries are difficult to read."
"Lesson is interrupted by announcement over intercom."
"One of the fluorescent lights starts to hum loudly."

An anecdotal record of these context events may help the teacher interpret certain behaviors of students (or of the teacher) that occurred during the lesson.

The anecdotal record consists of handwritten notes made by the supervisor as he or she sits unobtrusively somewhere in the classroom. Anthropologists often make handwritten ethnographic notes, too, but they have the option of using a portable audiotape recorder. As they make each observation, they simply make an audio-recorded description on the spot. This option is not usually available to a supervisor because he or she is physically too close to the teacher and students in the classroom.

Unless your handwriting is unusually legible, the anecdotal record will be difficult for the teacher to read and study. The preferred practice is to have your notes typed, so that the teacher has a neatly typed transcript to reflect on in the feedback conference. Also, a typed transcript has a more objective, neutral appearance than a set of handwritten notes.

### Example

Exhibit 8.1 presents a sample of an ethnographic protocol made by a professionally trained ethnographer.[2] It represents the rich descrip-

Protocol Number: 06
Name of Researcher: Gail
Date of Observation:
Subject of Observation:

    2nd Grade Class, Open
1. Classroom, with two team teacher
2. and two other adults.
3. This is a joint observation with
4. Elizabeth. I will be observing two
5. reading groups today, simultan-
6. eously, including 9 children. Out of
7. the nine children, 2 are girls, 7 are
8. boys.

8:30 Noise level 2
10. At 8:30 the noise level is 2. The
11. children have just been let into the
12. classroom, taking their coats off
13. and wandering around the room.
14. Several boys are in the corner
15. fighting, and some girls are sitting
16. on the floor playing a puzzle. The
17. teacher is walking back and forth in
18. the back of the classroom not at-
19. tending the children. The noise
20. continues and the children are run-
21. ning around. There is much con-
22. fusion in the room. Two teachers
8:35 23. stand at the desk talking to one
24. another. At 8:35, Mrs. Tyler
25. leaves the room. The team teach-
26. er stays seated behind the class-
27. room at her desk. At 8:40 Mrs.

28. Tyler comes back into the room.
29. She walks to the desk at the far
30. left hand side of the classroom,
31. which is a round table, and sits
32. on the edge. She says "Blue
33. Group, get your folders and go up
34. in the front, Green Group, come
35. here." Noise levels drop to 1, and
36. the children begin to follow her
37. orders. She says, "Anybody lose
38. a quarter?" No one responds, and
39. she repeats the question again
40. with irritation in her voice. She
41. says I know someone found.
42. someone lost a quarter because
43. it was found in the coat room.
44. Look in your pockets and see."
45. No one says anything.
46. She now stands up and pulls a
47. pile of workbooks from across
48. the table over to her. They are
49. the    reading workbooks.
50. She opens one of them on the
51. top and says, "Ah Daniel!" She
52. says this with a loud sharp voice.
53. She continues, "Your work yes-
54. terday was not too bad but you
55. need some work. Evidently there
56. are still some words you don't
57. understand." She thumbs through
58. the rest of his lesson. Danny is
59. standing at the outside of the cir-
60. cle around her, not listening to

61. what she is saying. Mrs. Tyler
62. now stands and gives instructions
63. to the Green Group. She tells
64. them to go through 8 through 13,
65. reading the two stories between
66. those pages and to go over the
67. work in the workbooks that she is
68. about to give back. She tells them
69. that they may seat any place but
70. not together and she says, "And I
71. don't want any funny business."
72. She now opens the next work-
73. book which is Nicole's. She tells
74. Nicole that she is having the
75. same problem that Danny is hav-
76. ing without specifying further.
77. Nicole looks up at her with an ex-
78. pectant look on her face. She
79. then looks at a third book and
80. says "Michelle, you're having the
81. same problem." She says,
82. "Snatch means to grab. Beach.
83. what does it mean?" Michelle
84. doesn't answer. She has her fin-
85. ger in her mouth and looks anx-
86. ious. The teacher closes the
87. workbook and pushes it to
88. Michelle. Michelle takes it and
89. walks away, with Nicole. Teacher
90. then opens the next workbook
91. and says, "Mike, I don't appreci-
92. ate all these circles. She points

**Exhibit 8.1. A sample protocol**

tion possible with this method. Anecdotal records made by clinical supervisors do not usually have the same amount of detail, although this is possible if the supervisor becomes proficient in quick note taking.

You might observe in exhibit 8.1 that the ethnographer does not focus on a particular child or a particular category of teacher behavior. The ethnographer instead records any salient event as it occurs. In this particular protocol the salient events seem to relate to the teacher's management and direction-giving techniques. The teacher can review the protocol to determine whether she wishes to maintain or change these techniques.

## Video and Audio Recordings (Technique 15)

Video and audio recordings are probably the most objective observation techniques. They allow teachers to see themselves as students see them. Another advantage of recordings is that they have a wide focus. They can pick up a great deal of what teachers and students are doing and saying. A good recording captures the "feel" of classroom interaction.

Video and audio recorders are becoming increasingly accessible as supervision tools. Not too many years ago these devices were expensive and bulky. Their cost, especially the cost of audio recorders, is now well within the reach of educational institutions. Unfortunately, video and audio recorders are used infrequently in teacher supervision even when the equipment is available. Video recorders are much more likely to be used in the coaching of school sports. Athletes and their coaches spend hours analyzing films or video recordings of games and individual player actions. Shouldn't we spend a fraction of our supervisory time with teachers reviewing recordings of their classroom interaction?

The portable video recorder is an integral component of the microteaching method.[3] Microteaching, which was developed at Stanford University in the 1960s, is widely considered to be an important innovation in the training of teachers. In microteaching the teacher practices a few specific teaching skills in a scaled-down teaching situation involving a ten- or fifteen-minute lesson with five or so students. The microteaching lesson is videotaped and played back to the teacher so that his or her teaching performance, especially the use of target skills, can be analyzed.

Teachers almost invariably find that the video recording provides an important self-learning experience. Nevertheless, there are several problems to avoid. First, supervisors must be careful to arrange the video recording equipment so that it does not interfere with the lesson. This is best done by setting up the equipment ahead of time, before students enter the classroom. Second, our experience indicates that teachers, when first exposed to a videotape of themselves, tend to focus on the "cosmetics" of their performance (e.g., physical appearance, clothes, and voice quality). In fact, a study by Gavrial Salomon and Fred McDonald revealed that in a videotape replay situation, 58 percent of teachers' self-observations were concerned with physical appearance, and only 18 percent were focused on teaching behavior.[4] This is a natural reaction. Ways to deal with it are suggested later in this section.

Another problem is that some teachers initially are anxious about the prospect of being videotaped. This problem can be alleviated by allowing teachers to experiment with the equipment before the classroom lesson is to be videotaped. Another helpful procedure is to allow a teacher to keep his or her own videotape or show the teacher how to erase the video recording. This calms any fear that the video recording might get into the "wrong" hands.

Although video recordings would seem to be a more powerful observational tool than audio recordings, this may not be so. Teachers sometimes are captivated by the image on the TV screen and do not listen to what is being said. Audio recordings have fewer distracting cues, and so it is easier for the teacher to concentrate on the verbal interaction. Research has shown that video and audio feedback are equally effective in helping teachers improve their use of verbal teaching skills.[5]

### Technique

The first step in making audio or video recordings is to obtain equipment that is in good working order. The portable video recorder typically includes a TV camera, a microphone, a videotape recorder (VTR), either reel-to-reel or cassette, a viewing screen, which may look like a regular TV set or be built into the camera, and cables for connecting the various components of the system. In addition, a supply of videotapes is needed.

We suggest that you find a free room where the equipment can be used and stored, especially if more than one teacher's classroom is to be videotaped. Perhaps later the same day, or the next day, each teacher can use the room to view the videotape replay.

Audio recorders are simple to set up and operate. Many self-contained models include a built-in microphone and operate on batteries. These recorders usually are designed for audio cassettes, which contain the audiotape and pickup reel in a small enclosed unit.

The recording process becomes more complicated as the size of the class increases. It is much easier to video-record or audio-record a group of five students than a group of thirty students. Most microphones for audio and video recorders have a small pickup range. As the focus of supervision is usually the teacher, we suggest that you place the microphone fairly close to the teacher. By doing so, you are likely to record everything the teacher says and some of what students say.

Teachers can learn to make their own video recordings, but in many situations it is more helpful if you, the supervisor, are present to make the recording. You need to find a convenient place to set up the camera on a stationary base; then, change the lens focus and turn the camera to follow the teacher as the lesson proceeds. Some systems allow you to make close-up recordings of events that interest you or the teacher by using a zoom lens.

A thirty-minute recording is usually more than adequate. It will try the teacher's patience and yours to play back a recording that is any longer than this. One procedure you can use is to have teachers play back the entire recording for themselves. They can share insights about their teaching performance with you during the feedback conference. At this time you can select a short segment of the recording (perhaps three to five minutes) for more intensive analysis. You will find that even a brief segment can yield many insights into the teacher's skill level and teaching style.

The wide focus of video or audio recordings is both a strength and a weakness. The insightful teacher will be able to observe many different aspects of teacher behavior and student behavior. Some teachers will notice only a few aspects, however, and may focus on the "cosmetic" features mentioned earlier. Your role in the feedback conference is to guide the teacher's observations, encouraging the teacher to draw inferences whenever possible, but also drawing the teacher's attention to significant classroom phenomena if they are being overlooked.

*Example*

Teaching Strategies is a required course in the secondary education program at the University of Oregon. Similar course content is part of teacher-education programs in many other colleges and universities. In Teaching Strategies students are asked to attend microteaching sessions in which they practice several different teaching methods. Students audio-record their lessons for later analysis. They also are required to make a transcript covering several minutes of the audio recording. This procedure ensures that students listen very carefully to what was said.

Exhibit 8.2 presents a partial transcript made by a student who had done a poetry lesson using the lecture method. This example shows that an audio recording and transcript made from it provided a rich source of feedback to the student on his teaching behavior.

Students in the Teaching Strategies course are also asked to write an analysis of their lesson based on the transcript and other feedback data. Exhibit 8.3 presents the first part of an analysis written by the student who gave the poetry lesson. It illustrates that the process of teaching a lesson and audio-recording it for later analysis is a powerful technique for helping the student see areas for instructional improvement.

Preservice teachers, including the one discussed here, tend to criticize themselves too severely in their initial encounters with self-audio recording. The supervisor can ameliorate this problem by reassuring students that flaws noted in their teaching performance are commonplace and can be eliminated with practice.

## A Global Screen (Technique 16)

An observation category system developed by the Central Educational Regional Laboratory for Illinois (CERLI) takes a broad look at teaching and provides a means for sorting out some common dimensions. Teachers commonly *seek* (S), *inform* (I), *accept* (A), and *reject* (R) facts, ideas, feelings, behavior. Hence, the CERLI instrument charts seeking, informing, accepting, and rejecting behaviors of the teacher across four categories involving students: cognitive (C), critical thinking (T), emotion (E), and classroom management (M). The resulting four-by-four grid allows the observer to tally the frequency of behaviors that fit the 16 categories produced by the combinations: SC, ST, SE, SM; IC, IT, IE, IM; AC, AT, AE, AM; RC, RT, RE, RM (see figure 8.1).

*Interesting*

0:00    OK, um, what I want to talk about is, uh, a poem by Denise Levertov, called "Living." (pause) And the reason I wanted to talk about this is because I think it's something that I can cover in 10 minutes, and uh, well, not in, not entirely but it's short enough to go over the basics, and, uh, Denise Levertov I, I think is, is . . . one of the

0:30    greatest of living poets, and not, not as well known as she should be. This poem in particular I think is, is, uh, one of her greatest poems, and it's not as well known as many, many poems that aren't nearly as good. (pause) Um, what I want to do is, is, is approach the poem in

1:00    terms of how it's organized . . . 'cause that's one way to get a grip, a grasp on a poem and Uh, not so much talk about what it says as, as the way it's, the way it's set up, um, and I, I don't think that's the only way to read a poem, in fact I don't think it's a very complete way but it's, um, it can lead you farther into a poem sometimes than

1:30    just talking about what it's about. And so let me just start with the way it sounds to me: "The fire in leaf and grass/ so green it seems/ each summer the last summer.// The wind blowing, the leaves/ shivering in the sun,/ each day the last day.// A red salamander/ so cold and so/ easy to catch, dreamily// moves his delicate feet/ and long tail. I hold/ my hand open for him to go.// Each minute the last minute."

2:00    (Pause) OK, um, it seems to me that that poem holds together very well. It's, it's a very tightly knit poem. Um. But it's not held together in any of the, the traditional ways: it's not, it doesn't have a rhyme scheme, there's no beat or rhythm that carries you along.

2:30    And so if you look at it — Well, does everybody agree that, that, it doesn't, it doesn't seem like a fragmented poem? It goes, it goes along, and I think it builds, builds very strongly towards its conclusion. Um . . . to start with, to start with the smallest units, just to

3:00    look at the sounds of the poem, and the way it . . . the way the sounds hold together — Starting in the first line: the, the first significant word is "fire." And you see that the "f" sound is repeated immediately in "leaf." And the "r" sound in "fire" carries forward into "grass," which then carries you forward into "green" again, and then down to the

3:30    "r" ending in "summer" and "summer" which is repeated. And then you see these, the "r" sound particularly you find again down in the poem down in the the uh, in "shivering" which repeats the "er" sound from "summer"--and that turns up again in "salamander" in the last, next to last triplet. And then the, when you get into "leaf" the, the

4:00    "ea" sound from "leaf" is repeated twice in the next line in "green" and in "seems"--and in "each" and in "leaves" in the next, the next stanza, and then, then you hear it again in "each"--in "easy"--in "dreamily"--in "feet"--and then again in "each" in the last line.

4:30    (Pause) And, um . . . these, these sounds (pause) are, um--well, the, uh, the tying together of the, of the poem through the, through the, uh, the sounds in the words goes on throughout the poem. For instance: if you look for the "o" sound, you don't see it until you get into the poem, but it turns up towards the end. If you move down

5:00    toward, to the third verse, it starts coming in very strongly, in this in a line "so cold and so/ easy to catch"--then it turns up again in "I hold my hand open for him to go." And these, these are, these are, these are the significant sounds in the poem. And this, this technique that Levertov relies on very, very strongly in a lot

5:30    of her writing is called "assonance." Um, I--does, everyone know what the meaning of assonance is? There's, there's two, uh, basic techniques used, but a lot of modern poets--assonance

**Exhibit 8.2. Transcript of lecture micro-lesson**

Once a teacher has an idea of how much of the classroom interaction falls into these cells, a more detailed look can be taken at any which appear especially interesting or worthwhile using, for exam-

*It wasn't a disaster. I think the students in the group and I learned some things about poetry from it.* ↓

I would rate this lecture <u>as a disaster</u>, and this
for two main reasons which are not unrelated:
nervousness and poor organization. A sudden attack
of stage fright was for some reason quite
unexpected, and because I hadn't anticipated it I
hadn't written out any more than a general outline
of the points I wanted to cover. This, as it turned
out, was not enough to see me through. Some of the
faults in this lecture, such as the astonishing
number of "um's," "uh's," and stuttering repetitions
(e.g., "What I want to do is, is, is approach the
poem . . .") are simply signs of nervous excitement;
having heard tapes of myself in conversation, I know
these mannerisms are not always present, at least
not to this degree. These I can only expect to
correct by calming down a bit, but this I think I
will be able to do if I correct some of the more
fundamental mistakes I made this time around.

The most important thing missing from this lecture
is an introduction. Immediately upon hearing the
first questions after I finished, I was made aware
that I had left out the necessary background for
reading the poem. And even though biographical
information about the author, for instance, was not
what I was mainly concerned with, it would have
given students <u>some</u> context, which is a necessary
preliminary to any appreciation. A preliminary
statement of what the poem is <u>about, or perhaps
simply some lead-in remarks about summer days and
why some moments seem more alive than others, would
have been very useful.</u> And although before the
lecture I had wanted not to seem too schematic,
afterwards I realized that I needn't have worried:
and I now regret not having outlined ahead of time
the areas I was going to cover.

*Yes. This would help. A good Technique!* →

It now seems to me, also, that I went at the poem
exactly backwards: for some reason I began with the
smallest details, the sounds of the poem, and went
on to its larger structure before talking about its
over-all theme. This is absolutely perverse; it is
almost as if I had been trying to keep the main point
a secret until the last possible moment. Clearly, it
would have been better to begin with the most
general statements, and to proceed to the more
particular ones only after these landmarks had been
mapped out.

I feel that, even so, using a blackboard would have
improved things immeasurably. Not only could I have
communicated better by writing down a few terms like
"assonance" and by marking the repetitions of sounds
rather than simply listing them; but also I think it
would have helped simply to get everyone's eyes and
attention (not least of all my own) away from the
handout sheet <u>and out into a more central meeting
place.</u> I even think that just having something to do
with my hands would have put me more at ease.

*nice phrase* →

I only asked questions twice in the course of the
lecture, and both questions were almost rhetorical,
being put in such a way as to actually discourage a
response: the first one beginning "does everyone

agree . . ." and the second one beginning "does
everyone know . . ." There were several other places
in the lecture where a question would have been in
order: and all of the questions should have been
less leading, more open to genuine answers. This
constricted questioning is, again, at least partly a
function of nervousness; as is the fact that I
forgot to ask for questions at the end.

**Exhibit 8.3. Lecture micro-lesson evaluation**

ple, selective verbatim. One can also record teacher behavior in the
upper portion of the square; student behavior in the lower portion.

Teachers are often surprised to find that they have concentrated
their efforts in different categories from what they thought. Some
examples of teacher behaviors and their categories are:

| | |
|---|---|
| a question about facts | SC |
| a question requiring thought | ST |
| a question about feelings | SE |
| a question about student behavior | SM |
| a statement about facts | IC |
| a statement about a concept or theory | IT |
| a statement about the teacher's or the student's feelings | IE |
| a statement about classroom rules or student behavior | IM |
| praise or encouragement of a student's factual answer | AC |
| praise or encouragement of a student's thoughtful response | AT |

| | Cog | Think | Emot. | Mgmt. |
|---|---|---|---|---|
| **Seek** | SC<br>T ₩ II<br>S III | ST<br>T<br>S | SE<br>T<br>S | SM<br>T<br>S |
| **Inform** | IC<br>T<br>S | IT<br>T<br>S | IE<br>T<br>S | IM<br>T<br>S |
| **Accept** | AC<br>T<br>S | AT<br>T<br>S | AE<br>T<br>S | AM<br>T<br>S |
| **Reject** | RC<br>T<br>S | RT<br>T<br>S | RE<br>T<br>S | RM<br>T<br>S |

**Figure 8.1. Each of the sixteen boxes represents a particular kind of
verbal statement, question, or remark. The observer can simply tally (e.g.,
‾‾‾‾ 11) the number of times each occurs by the teacher or a student. Each
box is divided into two parts—*T* for teacher talk and *S* for student talk.**

| | |
|---|---|
| reinforcing a student's expression of feeling | AE |
| reinforcing a student's behavior | AM |
| telling a student his or her answer to a factual question is incorrect | RC |
| disagreeing with a student's idea | RT |
| denying or criticizing a student's expression of feelings | RE |
| criticizing or punishing student behavior | RM |

Student comments, questions, expletives, answers, criticisms, expressions of approval, and other remarks can, in like manner, be tallied in the appropriate boxes.

# Notes

1. David C. Berliner and William J. Tikunoff, "The California Beginning Teacher Evaluation Study: Overview of the Ethnographic Study," *Journal of Teacher Education* 27 (1976): 24–30.
2. Ibid., p. 25.
3. Dwight W. Allen and Kevin Ryan, *Microteaching* (Reading, MA: Addison-Wesley, 1969).
4. Gavrial Salomon and Fred J. McDonald, "Pre- and Posttest Reactions to Self-Viewing One's Performance on Videotape" (paper presented at the annual meeting of the American Psychological Association, 1968).
5. Meredith D. Gall et al., "Improving Teachers' Mathematics Tutoring Skills Through Microteaching: A Comparison of Videotape and Audiotape Feedback" (paper presented at the annual meeting of the American Educational Research Association, 1971).

# 9

# Checklists and Timeline Coding

The man who can make a hard thing easy is the educator.
—*Emerson*

The observation instruments described in the previous chapters are relatively unstructured. In using selective verbatim, the SCORE techniques, anecdotal records, or video and audio recordings, teacher and supervisor jointly decide the categories of behavior to be observed. Occasionally, as a supervisor, you may wish to use a more highly structured instrument to observe behavior. You may prefer such instruments, or perhaps a particular instrument is well suited for your immediate purpose.

In another chapter we presented several checklists that teachers self-administer to identify their concerns about teaching. Now we present checklists that students complete to give feedback to their teachers, and checklists that the supervisor completes while observing a teacher's classroom behavior.[1] In addition, we describe a special checklist procedure called "timeline coding" that is useful for detecting patterns in classroom events.

## Student-Administered Checklists

As students participate in class, they have the opportunity to make extensive observations of their teacher's behavior. Summaries of students' observations can be useful in clinical supervision because teachers often are very concerned about how their students perceive them (even more than they are concerned about how supervisors perceive them!).

### Pupil Observation Survey (Technique 17)

The Pupil Observation Survey is a student-administered checklist that measures five different dimensions of teacher performance.[2] These dimensions reflect the extent to which the teacher

1. is friendly, cheerful, admired
2. is knowledgeable, poised
3. is interesting, preferred to other teachers
4. uses strict control
5. uses democratic procedure

The 38 items of the Pupil Observation Survey can be used by students in fifth grade and higher. If you wish to use a short version of this checklist, the Student Evaluation of Teaching form is available. A copy of it is presented in exhibit 9.1.

### IDEA H Questionnaire (Technique 18)

The IDEA H (Exhibit 9.2) questionnaire was developed by Judith Aubrecht and Gerald Hanna at Kansas State University. It is designed for use with secondary school students and allows the teacher to indicate which aspects of the course are essential, important, and not as important to the teacher's goals (items 1–9). The forms are scored electronically, taking into account the teacher's priorities.

The items were selected, modified, and validated through field testing, and norms were established based on a sample of more than 1000 representative classrooms.

IDEA H avoids a common fault of many student reaction forms, that is, forcing all teachers into a Procrustean bed regardless of whether they are attempting to be didactic or heuristic, factual or conceptual, behavioral or humanistic. The feedback from the scoring center tells the teacher what items (behaviors) to emphasize or continue to use given the teacher's preferences as expressed in marking which of the first nine items are essential, important, or not so important to *this* teacher.

# STUDENT EVALUATION OF TEACHING

D. J. VELDMAN and R. F. PECK

TEACHER'S LAST NAME: _____

SUBJECT: _____

SCHOOL: _____

| CIRCLE THE RIGHT CHOICES BELOW |
| --- |
| Teacher's Sex:   M   F |
| My Sex:   M   F |
| My Grade Level: |
| 3   4   5   6   7   8   9   10   11   12 |

**DO NOT USE**

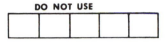

CIRCLE <u>ONE</u> OF THE FOUR CHOICES IN FRONT OF EACH STATEMENT.
THE FOUR CHOICES MEAN:

F = Very Much False
f = More False Than True
t = More True Than False
T = Very Much True

**This Teacher:**

F  f  t  T        is always friendly toward students.

F  f  t  T        knows a lot about the subject.

F  f  t  T        is never dull or boring.

F  f  t  T        expects a lot from students.

F  f  t  T        asks for students' opinions before making decisions.

F  f  t  T        is usually cheerful and optimistic.

F  f  t  T        is not confused by unexpected questions.

F  f  t  T        makes learning more like fun than work.

F  f  t  T        doesn't let students get away with anything.

F  f  t  T        often gives students a choice in assignments.

**Exhibit 9.1.   Pupil Observation Survey. Source: Research and Development Center for Teacher Education, The University of Texas, 1967.**

# iDEA ═══════ STUDENT REACTION TO COURSE AND TEACHER: IDEA FORM H

Your honest and thoughtful answers to the questions on this form can help your teacher improve this course and his/her teaching methods. Record all your responses on the separate answer card. Do not write your name on either this form or on the answer card. Your teacher will receive a summary of the responses of all students in your class, but should not know how any individual person answered.

---

**Part I.** Some of the things that students learn in school are listed below. For each, rate the amount of progress you have made in this course by marking the numeral of the most suitable response.

1 = None          4 = Much
2 = Little         5 = Great
3 = Medium

---

1. Gaining factual information (such as learning definitions, dates, vocabulary).
2. Understanding and applying principles, ideas, and theories.
3. Improving my learning skills (such as listening, reading, note-taking).
4. Improving my writing skills.
5. Improving my speaking skills.
6. Gaining skills and habits useful in everyday life or on a job.
7. Developing good feelings about myself (more acceptance of myself, more self-confidence).
8. Discovering or realizing my own interests, aptitudes, beliefs, and values.
9. Getting along with most other people.

---

**Part II.** For each of the following features of the course, fill in the numeral that best describes your reaction.

1 = Definitely not enough    4 = Too much
2 = Not enough               5 = Definitely too
3 = About right                 much

---

10. Amount of homework.
11. Number of tests.
12. Difficulty of reading.
13. Difficulty of course.

---

**Part III.** Describe your attitudes, feelings, and behaviors by filling in the appropriate numeral for each of the following statements.

1 = Definitely False       4 = More True than False
2 = More False than True   5 = Definitely True
3 = In Between

---

14. In general, I like my school teachers.
15. I am very glad it was this teacher who taught this course.
16. I try very hard to learn in all of my courses.
17. As a result of taking this course, I like this subject more.
18. I really wanted to take this course regardless of who taught it.

© Center for Faculty Evaluation and Development, 1981

---

**Part IV.** Indicate how well each of the following statements describes the students in this class by blackening the proper numeral.

1 = Definitely False       4 = More True than False
2 = More False than True   5 = Definitely True
3 = In Between

**The students in this class:**

19. Enjoy working together.
20. Are angry about grades.
21. Use their mistakes as opportunities to learn.
22. Take responsibility for their own learning.
23. Think they are wasting their time.
24. Are bored.
25. Have interesting and useful discussions.
26. Are rude and out of control.

---

**Part V.** Indicate how well each of the following statements describes your teacher by blackening the most suitable numeral.

1 = Definitely False       4 = More True than False
2 = More False than True   5 = Definitely True
3 = In Between

**This teacher:**

27. Understands student ideas and questions.
28. Expresses interesting and challenging ideas about the subject.
29. Uses tests, papers, projects, etc., that closely relate to the course purposes.
30. Cares about students as people.
31. Gives understandable explanations of course materials.
32. Asks interesting and stimulating questions.
33. Gives tests, projects, etc., that cover the important points of the course.
34. Shows interest in student ideas.
35. Speaks in an understandable voice.
36. Suggests clearer ways for students to express their ideas.
37. Gives quizzes, papers, projects, etc., that help students to learn.
38. Makes helpful comments about student work.
39. Reviews material in ways that help students remember it.
40. Gives projects, tests, or assignments that require original or creative thinking.
41. Creates opportunities for students to use the material they learn.
42. Makes helpful suggestions about what kinds of things to study for a test.
43. Shows how the subject relates to other areas of knowledge.
44. Speaks with expressiveness and variety.
45. Is sensitive to student feelings about the subject.
46. Provides helpful instructional materials (such as worksheets, study questions, unit objectives).
47. Identifies strong points of student work.
48. Uses good examples and illustrations.
49. Tries different ways of teaching when students have trouble learning.
50. Seems to enjoy teaching.

Exhibit 9.2

# Observer-Administered Checklists

As a clinical supervisor, you may choose to construct your own checklist for recording observations of classroom behavior. Here are several checklists we have constructed for our own use in supervision. You are invited to use them as is or to adapt them to your particular purpose.

### Question-and-Answer Teaching (Technique 19)

Question asking sometimes occurs when the teacher is introducing a new topic, but it is most often used to review curriculum materials students have just finished reading or seeing. For example, question asking may occur after students have read a chapter in a book, seen a film, completed a science experiment, or participated in a role-playing exercise.

The Question-and-Answer Checklist shown in exhibit 9.3 is organized around three types of behaviors. First are teacher behaviors that often lead to increased student participation in the lesson. Research shows that, unless teachers have received special training,

```
Behaviors That Increase Student
Participation
1. Calls on nonvolunteers
2. Redirects question
3. Praises student responses
4. Invites student-initiated questions

Behaviors That Elicit Thoughtful Responses
1. Asks higher cognitive questions
2. Pauses 3-5 seconds after asking a
   question
3. Asks follow-up questions to an initial
   response

Negative Behaviors
1. Reacts negatively to student response
2. Repeats own question
3. Asks multiple questions
4. Answers own questions
5. Repeats student's answer

Strong Points of Lesson

Suggestions for Improvement
```

**Exhibit 9.3.  Checklist for question-and-answer teaching**

they are likely to dominate the lesson by speaking two-thirds of the time. One technique to increase student participation is to call on nonvolunteers to respond. Teachers are likely to call on students who raise their hands and who customarily give good answers to their questions. Yet nonvolunteers often make good contributions if the teacher takes the initiative by calling on them.

Student participation also can be increased by redirecting the same question to several students. The teacher may invite additional responses to a question by a nod acknowledging a particular student or by a statement such as "Does anyone have a different idea?" or "Would someone like to add to what Susie said?" Praising answers is a technique that helps students feel that their answers are worthwhile; as a result, they are encouraged to speak up when other questions are asked. Another good technique is to ask students if they have any questions of their own about the lesson content. The teacher may choose to answer these student-initiated questions directly or may call on other students to answer them.

The second category in the Question-and-Answer Checklist refers to the cognitive level of the teacher's lesson. Educators generally agree that students should not just recite back the facts they have learned. (This is done by asking simple fact questions of the Who, What, Where, When variety.) Students also should be encouraged to *think* about the curriculum content. This goal is accomplished by asking higher cognitive questions, which are questions that cannot be answered simply by looking in the textbook. The student must think and formulate an original response. Higher cognitive questions may ask the student to compare and contrast, state possible motives or causes for observed phenomena, draw conclusions, provide evidence, make predictions, solve problems, make judgments, or offer opinions.

Asking a higher cognitive question may not be sufficient to elicit a thoughtful response. One helpful behavior is to pause several seconds before calling on a student to respond.[3] This gives students time to think. It also encourages all students in the class to generate an answer because they do not know whom the teacher will call on to respond.

The third technique for eliciting thoughtful responses on the checklist is to ask follow-up questions after the student has given an initial answer to a question. For example, the teacher might ask, "Did you agree with the jury's verdict?" and the student might respond, "No, I didn't." The teacher can follow up by asking the

BEHAVIORS TO BE TALLIED

Meaningful Content
1. Relates lecture content to content
   already familiar to students
2. Gives example to illustrate concept
3. Gives explanation for generalization or
   opinion

Student Involvement
1. Asks students if they have questions
2. Directs question to students
3. Has students engage in activity

BEHAVIORS TO BE RATED

| Organization | good | needs improve- ment |
|---|---|---|
| 1. Lecture has clear organization and sequence | 5 4 3 2 1 | |
| 2. Uses blackboard, handout, etc., to show organization of lecture | 5 4 3 2 1 | |
| 3. Tells students what (s)he expects students to remember from lecture | 5 4 3 2 1 | |
| 4. Repeats key points and summarizes them at end | 5 4 3 2 1 | |
| 5. Avoids digressions | 5 4 3 2 1 | |

| Delivery | good | needs improve- ment |
|---|---|---|
| 1. Speaks slowly and clearly | 5 4 3 2 1 | |
| 2. Conveys enthusiasm | 5 4 3 2 1 | |
| 3. Avoids reading from lecture notes | 5 4 3 2 1 | |
| 4. Avoids filler phrases such as "you know" | 5 4 3 2 1 | |
| 5. Avoids nervous gestures | 5 4 3 2 1 | |
| 6. Maintains eye contact with students | 5 4 3 2 1 | |
| 7. Uses humor | 5 4 3 2 1 | |

**Exhibit 9.4.   Checklist for lecture-explanation teaching**

student to support his position (e.g., "Why didn't you agree?"). Follow-up questions also can be used to encourage a student to clarify a vague answer (e.g., "I'm not sure I understood what you said. Can you restate your answer?"), to generate additional ideas (e.g., "Can you think of other ways of solving the energy crisis?"), or to challenge the student (e.g., "That's a good idea, but have you considered possible adverse consequences that might occur if your idea was put into practice?"). Follow-up questions can be used, too, to prompt a student who is unable to respond to the initial question.

The first two categories of behavior in the checklist in exhibit 9.3 refer to the "do's" of question asking. The third category refers to the "don'ts." Teachers should avoid reacting negatively to student responses by making critical remarks (e.g., "That doesn't make any sense at all") or by showing annoyance. Critical behavior only increases the likelihood that the student will volunteer no response in the future. The second negative behavior, repeating one's question, is to be avoided because it wastes class time and encourages students not to listen carefully the first time the teacher asks a particular question. The third "don't," asking multiple questions, refers to the practice of asking several questions in a row before settling on a question to which a response is invited. Teachers tend to do this when they are unsure of the lesson content or if they are inclined to think aloud. Multiple questions also waste class time, and they are likely to confuse students.

The final "don't" is repeating student answers verbatim. A better practice is to praise the answer, extend the answer by adding new information, or invite another student to build on the answer.

The bottom two headings of the checklist provide an open-ended opportunity for the observer to comment on strong points of the lesson and areas in which the teacher may need to improve.

### Lecture-Explanation Teaching (Technique 20)

As we have pointed out, research indicates that the average teacher does two-thirds of the talking in the elementary and secondary classroom.[4] The percentage is probably higher in some settings (e.g., college teaching) and lower in others. Much of this "talk time" is spent in presenting new concepts and information to students, or in explaining difficult parts of the curriculum. We have found that many teachers say they rarely use lecture as a teaching strategy when, in fact, much of their time is spent talking to students—

presenting new curriculum content or explaining ideas and procedures.

The checklist shown in exhibit 9.4 is designed for analyzing
various aspects of the teacher's lecture-explanation behavior. You
will note that the checklist is in two parts. The first part includes
behaviors that can be tallied each time they occur. The tallies are
counted to determine how often the teacher used a particular
lecture-explanation behavior during the lesson. Some of these
behaviors are techniques for increasing the meaningfulness of the
curriculum content—for example, the technique of giving examples
to illustrate a concept. Other behaviors are techniques for involving
students so that they do not sit passively through the entire lecture-
explanation. Asking students if they have questions about the lesson
is an example of a technique that usually creates student involvement.

The second part of the checklist is a list of teacher behaviors rated
by the observer. Some of the rated behaviors concern how well the
teacher organizes the lecture content. For example, repeating key
points and summarizing them at the end of the lesson is a technique
that helps students organize the various ideas in the lecture as
"more important" or "less important."

The largest category of behaviors in the checklist relates to the
teacher's skill in delivery. Lecture-explanation uses speech as its
medium, and so the teacher's mastery of oral delivery determines in
large part how well the curriculum content is conveyed to students.
The enthusiasm in the teacher's voice, the clarity of the teacher's
remarks, the avoidance of nervous gestures and filler phrases—all
contribute to the overall effectiveness of the lesson.

As in the Question-and-Answer Checklist (exhibit 9.3), this checklist can be augmented by including space for additional comments
about the strong points of the lesson and suggestions for improvement.

## Other Checklists

We have presented two checklists for observing two general strategies of teaching—question-and-answer and lecture-explanation.
Other checklists are available for observing more specific teaching
strategies. For example, Bruce Joyce and his colleagues present rating checklists for observing teaching strategies organized into three
models: information processing, social interaction, and personal.[5]

## Flanders Interaction Analysis

The best-known technique for classroom observation is the Flanders Interaction Analysis System.[6] This technique has been extensively researched and is widely used in teacher-training programs. It is called Interaction Analysis because the observation categories are used to record all verbal interactions that occur between teacher and students in a classroom setting. The record is analyzed to determine the verbal patterns that characterize the teaching style used by the teacher.

Our discussion of this technique is intended to familiarize you with its use in teacher supervision. Several excellent materials are available to help you acquire skills for using Interaction Analysis to make classroom observations.[7] It would certainly be worth your time to learn this technique in depth. We believe that you and the teachers under your supervision will find that it is a powerful tool for analyzing the act of teaching.

The Flanders Interaction Analysis System has two principal features: (1) verbal interaction categories, and (2) procedures for using the categories to make classroom observations.

The verbal interaction categories are shown in exhibit 9.5. You will note that, with the exception of category 10 (silence or confusion), all categories pertain to a specific type of verbal behavior. Any verbal statement that might be made by a teacher or student can be classified into one of the ten categories. This is true irrespective of grade level, subject area being taught, or personal characteristics of the teacher and students. Indeed, one of the major appeals of Interaction Analysis to educators is its universality. The ten categories can be applied to virtually any teaching situation. For example, a first-grade reading group and a graduate-level seminar could be compared for similarities and differences using the system.

You will note in exhibit 9.5 that the categories are classified into two kinds. Some verbal behaviors are responses a teacher might make to a student comment (categories 1, 2, and 3) or responses a student might make to a teacher comment (category 8). Other verbal behaviors are intended to initiate communication. Either a student (category 9) or the teacher (categories 5, 6, and 7) can play the role of initiator. Categories 4 and 10 are neutral. They reflect neither response nor initiation.

Another way of grouping the ten categories into larger units is to consider who is the speaker during a particular verbal interchange. In a classroom situation, the speaker is either the teacher or a

## FLANDERS INTERACTION ANALYSIS CATEGORIES* (FIAC)

| | | |
|---|---|---|
| **Teacher Talk** | Response | 1. Accepts feeling. Accepts and clarifies an attitude or the feeling tone of a student in a nonthreatening manner. Feelings may be positive or negative. Predicting and recalling feelings are included.<br><br>2. Praises or encourages. Praises or encourages students; says "um hum" or "go on"; makes jokes that release tension, but not at the expense of a student.<br><br>3. Accepts or uses ideas of students. Acknowledges student talk. Clarifies, builds on, or asks questions based on student ideas. |
| | | 4. Asks questions. Asks questions about content or procedure, based on teacher ideas, with the intent that a student will answer. |
| | Initiation | 5. Lectures. Offers facts or opinions about content or procedures; expresses his own ideas, gives *his own* explanation, or cites an authority other than a student.<br><br>6. Gives directions. Gives directions, commands, or orders with which a student is expected to comply.<br><br>7. Criticizes student or justifies authority. Makes statements intended to change student behavior from nonacceptable to acceptable patterns; arbitrarily corrects student answers; bawls someone out. Or states why the teacher is doing what he is doing; uses extreme self-reference. |
| **Student Talk** | Response | 8. Student talk—response. Student talk in response to a teacher contact that structures or limits the situation. Freedom to express own ideas is limited. |
| | Initiation | 9. Student talk—initiation. Student initiates or expresses his own ideas, either spontaneously or in response to the teacher's solicitation. Freedom to develop opinions and a line of thought; going beyond existing structure. |
| **Silence** | | 10. Silence or confusion. Pauses, short periods of silence, and periods of confusion in which communication cannot be understood by the observer. |

*Based on Ned A. Flanders, *Analyzing Teaching Behavior,* 1970. No scale is implied by these numbers. Each number is classificatory; it designates a particular kind of communication event. To write these numbers down during observation is to enumerate, not to judge, a position on a scale.

**Exhibit 9.5**

student.[8] Exhibit 9.5 shows that the first seven categories are used to code teacher statements. Categories 8 and 9 are for coding student talk. Category 10 reflects confusion or the fact that no one is speaking at a particular point in time.

The most critical distinction in Flanders's system is between response and initiation. If you think about the way in which you communicate with others, you will realize that you do one of two things: (1) respond to what someone else has said by listening or by offering a comment that directly relates to the other's communication, or (2) take the initiative by putting forth an idea, by giving a direction, or perhaps by criticizing what someone else has said or done.

When a teacher makes a responsive comment (categories 1, 2, or 3), he or she is said to be using an "indirect" style of teaching. You will note that these indirect behaviors are also associated with positive affect—accepting feeling, praising, and acknowledging students' ideas. When a teacher initiates a verbal interchange (categories 5, 6, or 7), he or she is said to be using a "direct" style of teaching. According to Flanders, asking a question is netural—neither direct nor indirect.

Student verbal behavior is summarized in two categories. The student is either responding in a narrow way to the teacher (category 8), or the student is expressing personal ideas and opinions (category 9). It is thought that a teacher's use of an indirect style of teaching (categories 1, 2, 3) encourages students to increase the frequency with which they offer their own ideas and opinions (category 9). In contrast, a teacher's use of a directive style (categories 5, 6, 7) is thought to channel students' ideas and behavior to meet teacher expectations (category 8).

This brief glimpse into Interaction Analysis reveals that it is both simple and complex. All classroom communication is coded into ten categories; yet, the data yielded by these categories can lead to complex analyses of the teacher's behavior. The intent of a teacher's communication can change from one second to another; these changes can form patterns that reveal a teacher's characteristic way of interacting with students. For example, one teacher's routine may be to ask a question (category 4), elicit a narrow student response (category 8), and respond in turn by asking a new question (category 4). This is a 4-8-4 pattern. Another teacher may be in the habit of asking a question, eliciting an open-ended student answer; then the teacher praises the student for the quality of the answer, builds on what the student has said, and initiates a new question. This is a 4-9-2-3-4 pattern.

As teachers are exposed to Interaction Analysis data on their classroom teaching, they are likely to move toward more complex and varied verbal behavior patterns. They also should become more aware of their verbal behavior and how it affects student learning.

At this point you have probably asked yourself, "Which is better—an indirect or a direct teaching style?" Research on Interaction Analysis suggests that use of an indirect teaching style is associated with more positive student attitudes and higher student achievement.[9] But this does not mean that a direct style is necessarily poor teaching. Flanders suggests that there are times in the curriculum when the teacher needs to be direct, as in presenting new content to students and in giving directions. In direct teaching, though, there is opportunity to use some indirect verbal behaviors. For example, the teacher may be giving an extended series of directions for doing an experiment (category 6). While doing this, the teacher might consider pausing to praise or encourage the students for their efforts and success in following directions (category 2).

A similar situation can occur in indirect teaching. For example, the teacher may be moderating a discussion in which students are encouraged to state their own opinions on an issue (category 9). The teacher may acknowledge students' ideas (category 3), encourage silent students to talk (category 2), and verbalize awareness of the feelings that underlie students' opinions (category 1). All these are indirect verbal behaviors. At some point in the discussion, though, the teacher may discover that students are misinformed about a particular issue and so decide to interrupt the discussion temporarily to provide information (category 5) and direct students to do homework reading (category 6). Thus, the teacher has interspersed direct teaching into a predominantly indirect, student-centered lesson.

We conclude this analysis of direct versus indirect teaching by advocating that teachers need to be *flexible*, as do supervisors (see chapter 11). They need to be able to use both direct and indirect verbal behaviors. A particular lesson may require a predominantly direct style, but the skillful teacher will find opportunity to use a few indirect behaviors as well. Another lesson may require a predominantly indirect style, but again the skillful teacher will find opportunity to interject new information and may find it necessary to direct students' ideas so that they are productive.

This is only a brief introductiuon to the ten categories of the Flanders Interaction Analysis System. We trust that it is enough to help you understand why these classroom observation categories have captured the attention of educators worldwide and why it has been used extensively in teacher supervision.

### Timeline Coding (Technique 21)   — *in relation to Flanders*

In describing Interaction Analysis, we stated that it has two main features. The preceding section discussed the first feature, namely, the ten categories for coding verbal behaviors. The other distinguishing feature is the way in which the behaviors are coded by the observer.

Exhibit 9.6 presents several examples of timelines used in conjunction with the Flanders Interaction Analysis System.[10] The first thing to notice about a timeline is its columns. Each column represents a three-second interval. The three-second interval is long enough that the observer need not become preoccupied with recording data. In most lessons there usually are several periods of time lasting a minute or more when only one interaction category is being used. (These are usually categories 4, 5, or 6.) The observer can relax during these time intervals until the pace of interaction increases again.[11]

The timelines shown in exhibit 9.6 have 30 columns for recording 30 discrete observations. Since an observation is made every three seconds, each timeline covers about one and one-half minutes of classroom interaction.

The other salient feature of an Interaction Analysis timeline is the rows. Each row represents one or two categories. The middle row is for teacher questions (category 4), which often are a stimulus for a series of interactions between teacher and students. Categories reflecting an indirect teaching style (1, 2, and 3) are above the middle row, as is the category reflecting open, student-initiated responses (category 9). Categories that indicate a direct teaching style (5, 6, and 7) are below the line, as is the category for structured, restricted student responses (category 8).

Category 10 (silence or confusion) is not represented by a discrete row. Tallies for this category are made below the timeline. Several categories (1 and 2, 6 and 7) share the same row in order to conserve space. The observer can use differentiated tallies (e.g., a check mark for category 1 and a slash for category 2) if he or she wishes to identify these categories separately on the timeline.

The organization of the Interaction Analysis categories on the timeline makes it easy for supervisor and teacher to detect verbal patterns that occurred during a lesson. For example, a majority of tallies above the middle row indicates that the lesson was indirect in style. A majority of tallies below the middle row indicates that the lesson was direct in style.

Exhibit 9.6. Timelines. (Copyright 1974, Far West Laboratory for Educational Research and Development, San Francisco, California. Published by Paul S. Amidon & Associates, Inc., 4329 Nicollet Avenue South, Minneapolis, Minnesota 55409.)

The first timeline in exhibit 9.6 is characterized by alternating 4s and 8s. This pattern suggests that the teacher was engaged in a rapid question-and-answer interchange with students, with the level of discourse probably focused on fact recall.

The second timeline in exhibit 9.6 suggests a richer, more indirect dialogue. The teacher starts by giving some information on a curriculum topic. Then students are invited to offer their own ideas on the topic. After each student response, the teacher takes care to acknowledge the student's idea and, in some cases, to praise it.

Many other interaction patterns can be revealed through timeline analysis. When teachers first become exposed to Interaction Analysis, they typically find that they use a few simple patterns in interacting with their students. As they see these patterns recorded on a timeline, they are likely to become dissatisfied and to explore how they can become more flexible in their use of verbal behavior. Sometimes, but not always, this involves a shift from a more direct to a more indirect style of teaching.

Our discussion of timelines has focused on its application to Flanders Interaction Analysis categories. Timelines are a generic recording device, however. With a bit of creativity on your part, you can imagine other behaviors that can be inserted in place of the Interaction Analysis categories (e.g., teacher feedback or teacher questions). Also, the three-second interval represented by the columns of the timeline can be varied. You may want a shorter or longer time interval depending on the observation categories included in your timeline system.

## Notes

1. Many other chekclists are described in Gary D. Borich and Susan K. Madden, *Evaluating Classroom Instruction: A Sourcebook of Instruments* (Reading, MA: Addison-Wesley, 1977).
2. The Pupil Observation Survey was developed at the Research and Development Center for Teacher Education, The University of Texas.
3. The importance of this teacher behavior is discussed in Mary B. Rowe, "Science, Silence and Sanctions," *Science and Children* 6 (1969): 11–13.
4. Ned Flanders, *Analyzing Teaching Behavior* (Reading, MA: Addison-Wesley, 1970).
5. These rating checklists are called Teaching Analysis Guides by Joyce and his colleagues. They are included in a set of three books: Marsha Weil and Bruce Joyce, *Information Processing Models of Teaching* (Englewood Cliffs, NJ: Prentice-Hall, 1978); Bruce Joyce and Marsha Weil, *Social Models of Teaching* (Englewood Cliffs, NJ: Prentice-Hall, 1978); Bruce Joyce, Marsha Weil, and Bridget Kluwin, *Personal Models of Teaching* (Englewood Cliffs, NJ: Prentice-Hall, 1978).
6. Flanders, *Analyzing Teaching Behavior.*
7. A brief, excellent package for learning how to use this observation system is *Interaction Analysis: A Mini-Course* by Ned Flanders and his

colleagues. It is available from Paul S. Amidon and Associates, Inc., 4329 Nicollet Avenue South, Minneapolis, MN 55409.

8. Some classes may have a guest speaker or a teacher aide. In this situation you may wish to adapt the Flanders Interaction Analysis System to accommodate the additional speaker(s).

9. See references on page 182.

10. The use of a timeline to record Interaction Analysis data is a relatively recent development. If you learned the system some years ago, you may be familiar, instead, with the use of matrices to record and interpret Interaction Analysis data. We present the timeline method here because we believe it is generally superior to matrices in ease of coding and interpretation.

11. When a simple interaction category occurs for any length of time, the observer may abbreviate the recordkeeping process. For example, if the teacher launches into an extended explanation of a concept, the observer may place a few tallies in the row designated by category 5, and then draw a short arrow with a note indicating approximately how many minutes or seconds this category of verbal behavior was used.

# Unit Exercises

Answers are on page 214.

**Multiple-Choice Items**

1. Teachers' use of redirection and probing can be analyzed by:

    *a.* the verbal flow technique.
    *b.* the at-task technique.
    *c.* the movement pattern technique.
    *d.* selective verbatim of teachers' questions.

2. Research has shown that the most common form of teacher feedback is:

    *a.* praise.
    *b.* criticism.
    *c.* repetition of what the pupil said.
    *d.* acknowledgment and elaboration of what the pupil said.

3. The figure shown to the right is most likely from a(n):

    *a.* selective verbatim record.
    *b.* verbal flow record.
    *c.* at-task record.
    *d.* movement pattern record.

4. The figure shown to the right is most likely from a(n):

    *a.* selective verbatim record.
    *b.* verbal flow record.
    *c.* at-task record.
    *d.* movement pattern record.

5. The specific emitters and targets of verbal behavior in classrooms can be identified most effectively by the:

    *a.* verbal flow technique.
    *b.* movement pattern technique.
    *c.* Student Perception of Teacher Style checklist.
    *d.* Flanders Interaction Analysis.

6. The technique most closely related to the ethnographic method in anthropology is the:

    *a.* video recording.
    *b.* timeline coding technique.
    *c.* anecdotal record.
    *d.* selective verbatim.

7. When first exposed to a videotape of their teaching behavior, teachers tend to focus on:

    *a.* their physical appearance.
    *b.* their students' physical appearance.
    *c.* their students' at-task behavior.
    *d.* verbal flow patterns.

8. The IDEA H Questionnaire and the Pupil Observation Survey are examples of:

    *a.* supervisor-administered checklists.
    *b.* teacher-administered checklists.
    *c.* school-principal-administered checklists.
    *d.* student-administered checklists.

9. In the Flanders Interaction Analysis System the behaviors of accepting feelings, praising, and accepting ideas are examples of:

    *a.* teacher initiation.
    *b.* teacher response.
    *c.* student initiation.
    *d.* student response.

10. In timeline coding columns are used to indicate _____, and rows are used to indicate _____.

    *a.* teacher initiation, student response
    *b.* teacher response, student initiation
    *c.* behavior categories, time intervals
    *d.* time intervals, behavior categories

## Problems

The following problems do not have single correct answers. Possible answers are on pages 216–17. Your answers may differ from ours, yet be as good or better.

1. A teacher under your supervision has a concern about how she

"comes across" to students but can't get any more specific than this in stating the concern. What observational techniques might you select? Why?

2. A teacher tells you he has several problem students in his class. The students create class disturbances and spend little time engaged in learning. The teacher would like you to collect data on their behavior that would help him better understand why these students are a "problem." What observational techniques would you consider using? Why?

3. On page 151 is a verbal flow chart made of an actual sixth-grade class. The teacher had given a presentation on a social studies topic and, at the time of the classroom observation, she was discussing the topic with the class. What inferences and recommendations for changes in the teacher's behavior might you make based on the verbal flow data?

4. The following is a transcript of the first few minutes of an actual lesson in a junior high school class. First, make a selective verbatim of the teacher's feedback statements. Second, code the transcript on a timeline using Flanders Interaction System. Assume that each line of the transcript represents a three-second interval.

($T$ = teacher, $S$ = student)

$T$: Who knows what a population explosion means? Who knows what it means?

$S$: I think it means like too many people, there's too many people living in like all over the world, there is just too many people. The population has just increased, the amount of people is just going up. It's just expanding, put it that way.

$T$: All right. How many people are here in the world right now?

$S$: A couple of billion.

$T$: A couple of billion. Any other guesses?

$S$: I'd say about six million.

$T$: Six million.

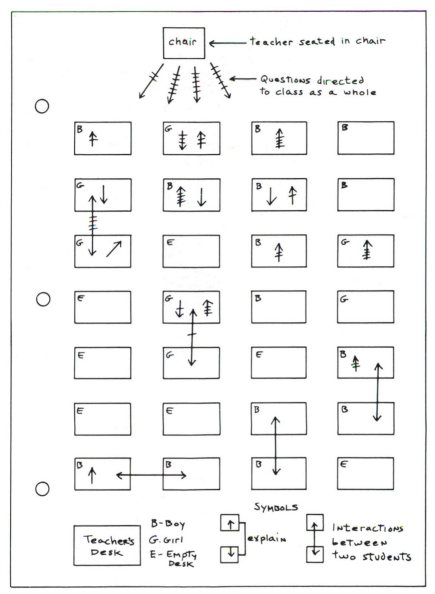

**Figure 9.1.**

S: There is only about a billion.

T: Only a billion.

S:   I'd say about three billion.

T:   About three billion. All right, Mary is closest because it is over three billion people in the world today. A couple of billion, that is a billion less than three billion, though, unless you meant a couple of billion or three. All right, what do they mean by squeezing to death? What do we mean by squeezing to death, Liza?

S:   Well, there will be so many people in the world that there will be no place for them to go, and they squeeze.

S:   Well, it means that there are a lot of people that are just barely making it in their life. You know, they don't have much money.

T:   All right, there are a lot of people that are just barely making it.

# Unit IV

# Conferences Based on Objective Data

## Overview

Data recorded by an observer must be shared with the teacher. Good data badly shared may become bad data. In this unit we look at some good ways to provide feedback to teachers, and we consider some of the interpersonal dynamics that are involved within the process. Chapter 10 is addressed to the feedback conference, and chapter 11 looks at direct and indirect styles of supervision.

## Objectives

The purpose of this unit is to help you develop:

Explicit techniques for providing useful feedback to teachers to aid them in analyzing, interpreting, and modifying their instructional efforts.

An approach to supervision consistent in style, strategy, and technique with the goals set forth in unit 1.

# 10

# The Feedback Conference

*You're the first one around here who has helped me.—Student comment*

Several things must have taken place before a successful feedback conference can occur.

1. In a planning conference, teacher and supervisor have set some goals for the year, identified concerns, established a rationale for working together, considered the strategies the teacher has been using and intends to use, and translated abstract concerns into observable behaviors the supervisor can record.
2. Before an observation session, teacher and supervisor have identified the nature of the lesson, made the objectives explicit, discussed what the teacher will be doing (strategy), predicted what the students will be doing (expectations), considered specific problems or concerns the teacher anticipated in the observed lesson, and selected appropriate observation techniques or recording systems.
3. During the observational visit the supervisor has employed one or more devices from a repertoire of data-recording techniques, has used appropriate recording devices for the specific situation as related to the goals and concerns, and has recorded data unobtrusively and without disruption of the class.

Now we are ready to begin a feedback conference.

The supervisor tries to provide objective observational data, analyze the data cooperatively, and reach agreement with the teacher on what is happening. Then teacher and supervisor interpret the data. The supervisor elicits the teacher's reactions to the data (inferences, opinions, feelings) and considers possible causes and consequences. Together, teacher and supervisor reach decisions about future actions. These may be decisions about alternative teacher strategies, different objectives for students, or modification of the teacher's self-improvement goals. At this juncture, teacher and supervisor may recognize a need for other kinds of information or make plans for the next observation. Often, the feedback conference for one observation becomes the planning conference for the next.

## Provide the Teacher with Feedback Using Objective Observational Data (Technique 22)

In one of our earliest workshops on observation and conference techniques, a principal remarked that making a chart of teacher movement seemed a strange thing to do. When given a chance to practice data gathering in an actual classroom, however, he tried a movement chart. He brought it back to the group, commenting on how much more *his* teacher had moved than had the teacher in our example. "And," he added, "the teacher looked at it afterward and said, 'This is really interesting information; you're the only principal who ever brought me something useful from an observation.'" The key to his unexpected success was that he had used the essential ingredient of effective conferences: providing objective data.

If the planning conference has established one or more goals that address genuine concerns and if the observational data are accurate and relevant, then the teacher should find the information useful, and the conference should run relatively smoothly. Many conferences are difficult because the data are "soft" (i.e., subjective, inaccurate, irrelevant). The inherent defensiveness teachers feel toward what they perceive as an evaluative situation is heightened by information that, to them, is suspect and debatable. "Hard" data alleviate this problem. Teachers do not say that what they saw on videotape or heard on audiotape did not happen, even though they may analyze or interpret events in a way that differs from the supervisor's analysis. Data in paper-and-pencil form (e.g., selected verbatim statements or seating charts) can be similarly convincing.

We should keep in mind, however, that all data are more or less subjective; even with videotape and film, someone chooses where to aim the camera and whether to take close-ups or long shots. Sound recordings can be affected by microphone placement and other factors. Checklists and charts are subject to the judgment, skill, and bias of the person tallying frequencies of given behaviors, choosing categories, or estimating qualitative ratings.

Similarly, in sharing information there is a temptation to add editiorial opinion either through direct comment or through a not-so-subtle use of adjectives. Consider this statement: "Here are some objective unbiased data on your chaotic classroom."

### Beginning the Conference

Having important information to discuss is the essential ingredient of a successful feedback conference. This means information that is objective (unbiased), accurate, clear (to both parties), relevant to the agreed-upon concerns, and interpretable in respect to what changes are feasible and reasonable. If the supervisor has this kind of information available in an easily displayed and readily understood form, a logical opening for the conference is "Let's look at the data we have collected."

*Analyzing* comes next, which means simply describing what the recorded information shows is happening without making value judgments. It is best for the teacher to take the lead in doing this.

*Interpreting* the data includes looking for probable causes of observed effects, or possible consequences, or suggested alternatives. Allowing the teacher to hypothesize several consequences or infer several reasonable causes of observed phenomena is usually a productive strategy. For example, repeated observations of student "at task" behaviors during a class period may show pupil interest in the activity waning after 20 minutes. The teacher may interpret this to indicate a weakness in the activity or a normal consequence of limited student attention span. Depending on the interpretation, decisions for change will vary. If the activity is judged inappropriate, it may be modified or changed substantially; if it is interpreted as appropriate but too long, it may merely need to be shortened.

*Deciding* what changes to make in future instruction can take many forms. Decisions can relate to any elements discussed in the planning conference. For example, the conferees may conclude that one or more of the following should be changed:

- the nature of the lesson or unit
- the objectives of the lesson or unit
- what the teacher does during the instruction
- what the students do during the instruction

- what additional kinds of information are needed to make intelligent decisions through analysis and interpretation

Another way of looking at decisions is to consider their magnitude. At one extreme, the teacher may decide to leave teaching as the result of systematic observational feedback (this has happened). At the other extreme, the teacher may decide not to change a thing (this has not happened, in our experience; teachers who believe they are perfect must be very rare). More often, teachers think of several aspects of the instruction that could be changed. The teacher may decide to experiment with these changes one at a time and analyze the effects. Usually the effects can be observed by the teacher without repeated visits by an observer, but in some cases an observer will be needed. In addition to the supervisor, other observers may be available—colleagues, aides, or even students.

Occasionally a teacher reaches a decision as the result of viewing data the supervisor provided without comments during the feedback conference. For example, a teacher may resolve to get rid of an annoying mannerism noted in watching a videotape or to spend more time working with a certain student after noting the student's behavior recorded on a seating chart observation record. One teacher, who was using a low-key style during a vieotaped observation, displayed a dynamic style during the next observation (also videotaped). When asked by the supervisor about the obvious and abrupt change in teaching style, a matter that had not been mentioned in the previous conference, the teacher replied, "It wasn't until after I saw that first tape that I realized how undynamic I was. I swore I'd try something much different the next time!" Such a radical change is unusual, but this teacher found he was capable of a more energetic approach to teaching—at least occasionally.

Science makes use of accurate data to understand, predict, and thereby control. Similarly, when presented with factual information rather than inferential conclusions drawn by the supervisor, the teacher is in a position to behave professionally and responsibly in the next step.

## Elicit the Teacher's Inferences, Opinions, and Feelings (Technique 23)

Providing objective data (technique 21) can be translated into practice as, "Here's what I recorded from your lesson; let's have a look at it." The technique we are about to discuss, eliciting reactions, does *not* call for an opening question like, "How do you feel your lesson went?" Cautious teachers hesitate to say, "Great!" for fear you will contradict or disagree. On the other hand, if they say, "Lousy," they run the risk of having you agree. "Some parts were good, others could be improved" is a safe answer, but this is what the conference is all about anyway. The supervisor can choose a less threatening opener, after the teacher has had a chance to inspect the information, by asking, "What aspects of the data do you want to talk about first?"

Eliciting the teacher's reactions to the data requires skill and patience. There is always a temptation to jump to conclusions about what has been observed and recorded before the teacher has had an opportunity to reflect on it. A device that works well, especially in connection with tape recordings, is to ask the following questions:

"What do you see [or hear] in the record [or tape] that you would repeat if you did this lesson again?"
"What would you change?"
"If you were a student in the class, what would you want to change?"

We have asked these questions of hundreds of teachers—primary, intermediate, secondary, and college teachers—who have viewed videotapes of themselves. No one has answered all the questions with "I wouldn't change a thing." If "What would you repeat?" gets no response, you can proceed immediately to the second question. If the teacher expresses total satisfaction with the lesson in response to "What would you change?" the third question, "What would a student want changed?" should provoke a more thoughtful response. The teacher can be asked to view the instruction from the perspective of different students, say, one who usually has difficulty understanding and one who is usually ahead of the rest.

These questions are phrased in a relatively nonthreatening manner to which most teachers are able to respond openly and with considerable insight. In response to the third question, one teacher said,

*T:* "Which student?"
*S:* "What do you mean, which student?"
*T:* "Well, the slowest, the brightest, the least interested?"
*S:* "OK, the slowest."

> *T:* "All right. What I see that teacher doing is talking too fast,
> using vocabulary I don't understand, discussing topics that
> don't affect me. I don't think she likes me; she never calls
> on me even when I know the answer."

This was a healthy insight for the teacher to develop, and the
anecdote points out that one function of the supervisor is to serve as
a catalyst, to help the teacher make productive use of the available
information.

For most teachers, the steps in the feedback conference are
reasonable and appropriate: providing objective data, analyzing and
interpreting it, and drawing conclusions with the teacher taking
equal part in a collaborative process. Unfortunately, many supervisors reverse the process. They provide their own conclusions, give
some analysis that justifies the conclusions, then search for data to
substantiate the analysis. Often, no alternative interpretations are
even considered.

For a small percentage of teachers a "conclusions first" conference
approach may be needed. For example, it may be more effective to
say, "You've been late for work twelve times this month. This has
got to stop, or else!" rather than to say, "Here are some data about
your punctuality. Do you find anything of interest?" An alternative
effective strategy could be "What do you propose to do about this
record of tardiness?"

There are several assumptions in a procedure that encourages
teachers to come to their own conclusions, based on objective information and thoughtful analysis:

- Few teachers set out deliberately to do a bad job. Most have
  reasonable goals.
- Most teachers have alternative strategies available and can use
  them if they see a need.
- We don't "see ourselves as others see us." Being able to view our
  teaching from a new perspective can be an enlightening experience.
- Those insights we discover for ourselves tend to be retained and
  acted on with more energy and better spirit than those we are
  told about by others.
- Many teachers prefer a collaborative, collegial approach instead
  of one in which the supervisor is regarded as "superior."
- Good data can be more persuasive than mere admonishments.

Persuasive data contain no value judgments. Inferences and generalizations the *observer* may have formed about the activity are not included in the data presented in a conference with the teacher. Data that might lead the teacher to the same inferences probably should be presented, however. Persuasive data, in addition to being value-free, must be specific and presented in a form that can be understood and used immediately by the teacher. They also must be data the teacher feels are necessary and important at a given time. For example, a teacher concerned about the inability to ask good questions is probably not ready for data and conferences designed to improve lecturing prowess. Or data that might be helpful to a teacher worried about disciplinary problems might be regarded as irrelevant by a teacher who has no problem with discipline. The observer needs a variety of skills to share data in a persuasive manner at a time when the teacher feels that the data are relevant, important, and useful.

One elementary teacher, after studying a seating chart on which an observer had recorded which students were responded to by the teacher (and in what ways), began to understand why some students felt "turned off" and planned activities that created opportunities to respond in positive ways to those students. Many teachers who have analyzed charts of their direct and indirect behaviors (using Flanders's categories) have modified the indirect-direct ratio. Teachers who have had access to verbal flow patterns on seating charts (who talks to whom) often have been stimulated to experiment with different seating arrangements.

A high school science teacher studied observational charts that showed what percent of his students were at task for various time periods. The percentages were strikingly high, which might have been expected to please this instructor. Yet the teacher concluded that they were too high. Every year a number of students dropped this course; after the instructor saw the data, he realized he was "keeping their noses to the grindstone" so much that the course was unduly punishing. He decided to restructure the course.

When a supervisor feels that a teacher is drawing acceptable inferences and suggesting reasonable alternative plans for the future, a simple reinforcement is all the technique needed. The supervisor can say, "That sounds like a good idea, Pat. Why don't you try it?"

Another teacher had been having some real problems with lesson preparation and control of students. She was observed on two successive days, the observer taking verbatim notes of her questions and control statements. At the feedback conference, the observer began the conference as follows:

S: "How do you feel about the two lessons?"
T: "Well, I feel that it went better today than yesterday. But how did I look?"
S: "You know I'm not going to answer that."
T: "I know."

It would have been better for the observer to start the dialogue with

S: "Here are the questions and control statements you wanted to analyze. Let's have a look at them."

If the teacher asks "How did I do?" an appropriate answer is "Let's see." Then teacher and supervisor turn to the data.

### Encourage the Teacher to Consider Alternative Lesson Objectives, Methods, Reasons (Technique 24)

Once a supervisor has analyzed the data, the tendency is to say to a teacher, "Here's what I would do if I were you." This short-circuits the system. If teaching were a straightforward physical skill, then viewing the performance and giving advice like "Keep your eye on the ball" would be effective. Translated to advice about teaching, this tends to become "Be firm, fair, and consistent." This is undoubtedly good advice, but it does not tell what to be firm about (discipline? standards? questionable rules? teacher opinions?) or what is fair and consistent for all (activities for the physically handicapped? individualized academic assignments?). Moreover, there are always feasible alternatives for teaching anything. When change is desired, one purpose of the feedback conference is to get the teacher to consider several alternatives and choose the most promising. Teachers should be able to give alternative explanations of why things might be happening the way they are and also to suggest several ways to change the situation, or the strategy, or the activities.

Student teachers and beginning teachers have a more limited repertoire of possible approaches than do more experienced teachers. One benefit accruing from systematic observation and teacher-centered conferences should be teachers who, on their own volition, do self-analyses using objective data and thus develop a wider range of alternative approaches.

For example, a group of beginning teachers in an intern program read about social-class discrimination by teachers in schools. They recorded their own interactions with students in their classes, played them back, and were surprised to learn that they, too, were favoring middle-class children.

Another group of inexperienced teachers asked for help in learning how to control student participation in recitations and discussions. They were asked to note several students who were often active participants in a lesson and several others who seldom participated. In the next lesson they were asked to see if they could limit those who talked the most to no more than three contributions and get those who rarely participated to make at least three contributions. Every teacher reported being able to accomplish this assignment without any special instructions; simply being aware of the two groups of students was all that was necessary.

Many aspects of teaching can be observed, recorded, and analyzed as easily as counting student contributions to a recitation or discussion. You may wonder why teachers are not more aware of such obvious patterns as paying more attention to one side of the room or calling only on students in the front seats. The answer is that these things are not obvious to teachers while they are preoccupied with the details of teaching. They are not obvious to observers either, unless they are watching for them.

Supervisors often feel that if they record specific information, such as the nature of the teacher's responses to individual students, they will miss other important elements of the teaching-learning situation. Our experience suggests that we see more as observers when we have something specific on which to focus our attention. Making an audiotape recording in addition to whatever charts or codes the observer is keeping on paper ensures backup information about the lesson if it is needed.

A common worry among beginning teachers is the problem of discipline. Students can get out of hand whether they are first graders or high school seniors. Feedback on this aspect of teaching can bring startling results. One of our practice teachers asked that we videotape her troublesome fifth-period class instead of the well-behaved first-period class we had taped twice before. She volunteered the tape for analysis in a seminar on a day when classroom discipline was to be discussed and a film was to be shown that

illustrated both ineffective and effective techniques. When her classroom tape was played later in the session, the teacher was able to
see herself using many of the ineffective techniques portrayed in the
film.

## Provide the Teacher with Opportunities for Practice and Comparison (Technique 25)

As a source of alternative teaching methods, a supervisor may be
asked to play a more direct role as a model for a teacher by demon-
strating a particular method or technique in the classroom. Curriculum specialists in particular are often asked to do such demonstra-
tions. When this is done, the teacher becomes the observer and
records data to be analyzed and interpreted in a postdemonstration
conference. For example, an elementary teacher was experiencing
difficulty explaining "pi" and the formulas $C = \pi d$ and $A = \pi r^2$. She
asked a mathematics specialist to take over a lesson while she
observed the explanation and recorded student questions. During
the feedback conference, information about the supervisor's lesson
was incorporated into information taken from the teacher's experience and plans.

Another frequent strategy is to suggest that one teacher observe
another in order to compare styles or strategies or pick up some
different techniques. If the observing teacher has some knowledge
of systematic observation and recording, the feedback conference
can result in a mutual sharing of ideas and perspectives.

Time for collecting information and providing feedback is always
limited. Most supervisors should spend more time on these activities than they typically do; even those supervisors who allot the
most time feel a need for more. One way to increase the amount of
feedback is for the teacher to collect some of it. This can be done
with teacher-made tape recordings (audio or video), by getting systematic feedback from students, or by using teacher aides or colleagues as observers.

When data come from sources other than the supervisor's
observations and are analyzed by the teacher without a structured
conference, some guidelines are needed. The supervisor can help
the teacher pick a central focus for the self-analysis. This can be one
of the goals for the year that the teacher and the supervisor set at
the first planning conference. Or it can be a concentration on a
certain technique the teacher wishes to strengthen, say, asking

better questions or moderating group discussions, giving clearer explanations and directions, or exhibiting more warmth and enthusiasm.

Care needs to be taken in selecting an appropriate source of information. For topics like those in the preceding paragraph, audio-tape recordings would be reasonable. Information about how instruction is being individualized might come from an adult observer or from the students themselves. Several instruments are available for collecting student feedback. The products of student work also can be analyzed in relation to the teacher's goals.

The teacher can incorporate self-analysis activities in a future feedback conference. For example, one teacher discovered a surprising and unsuspected number of "put-downs" in his informal interactions with students. He was determined to make several 10- or 15-minute tape recordings each week at times when he would be interacting informally with groups. The supervisor suggested that the teacher note the frequency of such remarks in the samples over time and write examples of what he had said along with alternative phrases he could have used. The next time teacher and supervisor got together, both were pleased with the progress that had been made. Moreover, they agreed it would be useful for the supervisor to check the perceptions of a few students informally.

Beginning teachers need systematic practice in using a variety of strategies and techniques. Many of these can be practiced without direct supervision and recorded for self-analysis. Here are some common strategies along with suggested means of self-observation.

| Strategy | Self-Observational Device |
|---|---|
| Lecture: explanations, directions | Audiotape recording, selective verbatim* |
| Discussion, seminar | Verbal flow chart* made by student or by teacher using tape recording |
| Demonstration | Videotape recording |
| Individualized instruction: seatwork, resource centers, laboratory, shop | Classroom traffic (movement) chart* drawn by aide. |
| Simulations, games, self-instructional materials | At-task chart* prepared by teacher as students participate |

*These devices are described in unit III.

| Heuristic approaches: problem solving, inquiry lessons, guided discovery | Selective verbatim of teacher questions or student questions taken from tape recording |

If the teacher has collected and analyzed some of the data, much time can be saved in a subsequent conference with the supervisor. Some tasks the teacher can perform also will make the teacher better informed at the time of the conference. For example, transcribing selected verbatim from a tape, charting student participation, or plotting frequencies from a student questionnaire will make the teacher aware of elements that need improvement or emphasis.

The feedback conference can also be shortened if the supervisor provides the teacher ahead of time with the data that will be discussed. It is often convenient to make a carbon or photocopy when data are being recorded. After the lesson, the observer can say to the teacher, "Here's a copy of the raw data. Look it over before we meet, and I'll do the same."

## Summary

In this chapter we have described the techniques essential to a clinical supervision feedback conference:

*Provide the teacher with feedback using objective observational data.* If the data are inadequate, inaccurate, biased, or irrelevant to the teacher's concerns, the process cannot get started. The teacher must feel that the information being analyzed is a valid representation of what is really happening in the classroom. Information that relies on memory is less persuasive than information that is objectively recorded.

*Elicit the teacher's inferences, opinions, and feelings about the observational data.* If the data are accurate and objective, but the supervisor immediately draws opinionated inferences from the data, the teacher may feel compelled to respond defensively rather than interpret the data in a self-directed and productive way. It takes self-control and practice to provide another person with data in a nonevaluative, nonthreatening manner. The use of adjectives or nonverbal cues may communicate opinions or conclusions to the teacher before he or she has had a chance to work through the steps.

3) *Encourage the teacher to consider alternative lesson objectives, methods, reasons.* If the teacher expresses dissatisfaction with something observed in the lesson, several reasonable hypotheses may help explain why an event is occurring; it is a mistake to zero in on only one possibility. Similarly, several feasible alternatives are usually available for dealing with a problem; more than one should be considered before settling on the best alternative. Here the supervisor can help the teacher avoid two traps: (1) "functional fixedness," proceeding to judge all information on the basis of a single hypothesis (which may be wrong); and (2) "a working definition of insanity," considering only one solution to a problem and when that doesn't work, doubling and redoubling our efforts with the same unsuccessful approach. The collaborative setting of the conference should provide teacher and supervisor with a wider range of hypotheses and proposed solutions than either conferee could generate alone.

4) *Provide the teacher with opportunities for practice and comparison.* Because the teacher has settled on a plan of action, the supervisor should not expect to see the problem solved immediately. Teachers need time to try out new approaches, develop new skills, or compare several strategies. The supervisor can follow up at a later time to observe, record, and reinforce teacher progress.

Ideally, the feedback conference takes the following form:

1. The observer *displays* the data recorded during the observation. This is done without evaluative comments.
2. The teacher *analyzes* what was happening during the lesson as evidenced by the data. The supervisor simply helps to clarify what behaviors the recorded data represent.
3. The teacher, with the help of the supervisor, *interprets* the behaviors of teacher and students as represented by the observational data. At this stage the teacher becomes more evaluative because causes and consequences must be discussed as desirable or undesirable.
4. The teacher, with assistance (sometimes guidance) from the supervisor, *decides* on alternative approaches for the future to attend to dissatisfactions with the observed teaching or to emphasize those aspects that were satisfying.
5. The supervisor *reinforces* the teacher's announced intentions for change when the supervisor agrees with them or helps the teacher modify the intentions if there is some disagreement.

Supervisors are often surprised at how easily these steps can be accomplished. When supplied with adequate information and allowed to act on it, most teachers can analyze, interpret, and decide in a self-directed and constructive manner. When things do not go well in a feedback conference, the difficulties can usually be traced to failure on the part of the supervisor to use an effective clinical supervision technique.

# 11

# Direct and Indirect
# Styles of Supervision

Take my advice: don't give advice.—*Anonymous*

The techniques in chapter 10 can be used by any supervisor who has systematically collected observational data to analyze with a teacher. How the data are interpreted and what decisions are reached will depend to a considerable extent on the supervisor's style. Styles of supervision can be described in many ways; we shall use a common distinction: direct versus indirect styles.

Flanders[1] differentiates direct teaching styles (i.e., lecturing, directing, criticizing) from indirect styles (i.e., accepting feelings, encouraging, acknowledging, using student ideas). Blumberg[2] uses similar categories for supervisor behavior and has gathered some evidence that teachers prefer an indirect style of supervision.

The direct and indirect behaviors a supervisor may employ can be placed on a continuum, though no scale is intended.

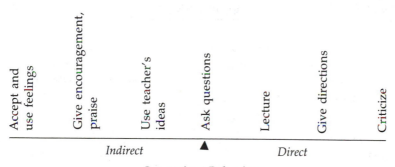

**Supervisor Behaviors**

Another range of possible conference behaviors on the teacher's part can be constructed using the work of Spaulding.[3]

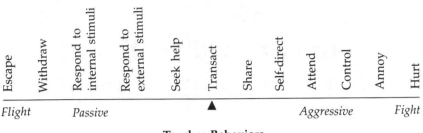

**Teacher Behaviors**

The behavior of either conferee can be described with labels used by Shostrom.[4]

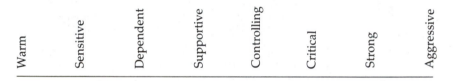

**Characteristics of Conferees**

These characteristics can be translated into verbs that describe a range of verbal behavior the supervisor or teacher can employ.

| Care | Guide | Appreciate | Empathize | Respect | Express | Lead | Assert |
|------|-------|------------|-----------|---------|---------|------|--------|

One can also view the supervisor's actions as aversive (dominative, punishing) or supportive (approving, receptive). Setting limits and setting goals are actions that usually lie between these extremes but can be pushed toward one end or the other.

| Approving | Receptive | Setting Goals | Setting Limits | Dominating | Punishing |
|-----------|-----------|---------------|----------------|------------|-----------|

*Supportive*                                                                                     *Aversive*

Although teachers indicate a preference for supervisors who emphasize the supportive, caring style, these are not the only appropriate behaviors for a supervisor. A caring style at times may be indicated by doing something aversive (e.g., when a parent prevents a child from playing on the highway).

This chapter recommends several techniques usually regarded as indirect, but they also can be used by direct supervisors. Indeed they should be so used when persuasive data are shared. The techniques are concerned with listening, acknowledging, clarifying, encouraging, guiding (rather than directing), supporting, and dealing with feelings.

The techniques that follow are especially useful for supervisors who want conferences to be "teacher-centered." Whether a supervisor's essential style is direct or indirect, self-centered or teacher-centered, these techniques can be used to improve the quality of interaction between the conferees.

## Listen More, Talk Less (Technique 26)

Many supervisors dominate the conversation. The teacher has little chance to identify goals and objectives, analyze and interpret information, or reach decisions about future actions. Teachers talk to students about two-thirds of the time they teach, and supervisors talk in about the same proportion to teachers. The exact ratio varies, but too many supervisors do most of the talking. It is difficult to attend to a teacher's concerns in a conference or encourage a teacher's plans for improvement when the supervisor monopolizes the conference. Avoid this tendency when applying the techniques in the remainder of this chapter.

## Acknowledge, Paraphrase, and Use What the Teacher Is Saying (Technique 27)

Supervisors who insert an "I understand" or "I know what you mean" in the course of a teacher's conversation indicate that they are listening. Accurate paraphrases also show that they understand the teacher. Using the teacher's ideas can be even more convincing than merely acknowledging (hearing) or paraphrasing (comprehending) them. Applying an idea to a different situation is but one example; pointing to a logical consequence is another. Paraphrasing can be overdone if too many responses are similar, or if they are inappropriately placed. For example, if a teacher says, "The car was going sixty miles an hour," it doesn't contribute much to respond, "What you are saying is that the automobile was traveling a mile a minute." An effective paraphrase must be a genuine effort to communicate that we understand what the other person is getting at. Using an idea of the teacher's shows that the supervisor heard, understood, and is pursuing the thought. Of course, it can be pursued so far that it ceases to be the teacher's idea and becomes the supervisor's. Generally, however, having a person you respect use your idea is rewarding.

### Ask Clarifying Questions (Technique 28)

The teacher's statements often need to be probed to clarify the supervisor's understanding and to get the teacher to think carefully about inferences and decisions. "Tell me what you mean by that" or "Can you say a little more about that?" are examples. So are "What would you accept as evidence that _____ is happening?" "Do you know someone who is especially good at that? What does he do?" "Would you give me a specific example?"

In many instances, if we do not clarify, miscommunication is the result. Occasionally someone will say, "You're absolutely right! Moreover,..." Any then the person proceeds to say the exact opposite of what you thought you said. Of course, that also could be a conscious strategy or a case of not listening at all, but a clarifying question avoids unintentional misunderstandings.

An example of paraphrasing and asking clarifying questions took place in a high school where the principal gave the faculty an administrator appraisal form to fill out anonymously. After analyzing the compiled responses, the principal said in a faculty meeting, "What you seem to be telling me in this survey is that I'm not as accessible as you would like." Several teachers said, almost in unison, "Could you tell us what 'being accessible' would look like?" To which the principal replied: "Well, I'd keep my door open more and welcome 'drop-in' chats. And if you stopped me in the hall and asked a question, I'd try to answer it briefly instead of pointing out that I was on my way to a meeting."

Having announced and clarified his intentions in public, he was destined to become "Mr. Accessible" in the next few months. Of course he had some help from wags on the faculty who could not resist asking, "Are you feeling accessible?"

Several points can be made with this example: (1) the paraphrase translated a statistic into flesh-and-blood behavior, (2) the clarifying question checked the perceptions of the subject and his observers, and (3) the public announcement of a resolution to change virtually ensured success. The same process takes place in the feedback conference. Note that the principal had objective data, analyzed and interpreted the data, made a decision, made use of paraphrasing and clarifying questions, and received verbal support in his resolve to change. These are exactly the steps we should follow in helping teachers improve their teaching.

## Give Specific Praise for Teacher Performance and Growth (Technique 29)

To say "That was a nice lesson" is not specific praise. Saying "That was an excellent answer you gave to Billy" or "Removing Fred from the group was an effective way to handle the problem" makes the approval explicit. It is especially important to note positive instances where the teacher has shown growth toward an avowed goal.

There is some possibility that a supervisor will reinforce more than was bargained for. A workshop leader received this comment from a participant on the postworkshop evaluation: "Stopping the tape recording to explain what was happening was really helpful." So the leader stopped the tape about 20 times during the next workshop, until someone sent this note: "Why don't you let the tape play long enough for us to hear what's going on?"

Again, an elderly lady who had never eaten apple pie remarked that when she was a girl, she turned down her first opportunity to do so and gained considerable attention: "Imagine that! Carrie doesn't eat apple pie." The attention was such that in subsequent situations, she felt compelled to continue her refusal, although she confessed, "I always thought I might have liked it."

Yet in our experience, the possibility of too little reinforcement for teachers is much more likely than too much. Teaching often seems a thankless task to those who toil in the schools of our nation. They seldom lack critics, however.

## Avoid Giving Direct Advice (Technique 30)

This does not say *never* give direct adivce, just wait a while. Let teachers analyze and interpret. Often the decisions they reach will be very similar to yours. For most teachers, having their ideas for change reinforced by someone they respect is more likely to produce results than having to carry out someone else's idea. On the other hand, there are times when it is better to say what we think rather than let indirectness become manipulative.

Some people are naturally compliant, submissive, obedient; perhaps they enjoy being told what to do. Nevertheless, our experience with teachers indicates that most of them prefer to feel responsible for their own actions. People who choose teaching as a career expect to be in charge of their classes; they expect to make professional decisions about goals, subject matter, materials, methodology, evaluation, and other aspects of the educational process.

The line between "guided discovery" and "manipulation" is a fine one. The supervisor must decide when "Here's the way it looks to me" is preferable to making the teacher feel that guessing games are being played.

## Provide Verbal Support (Technique 31)

The emphasis of the supervisor is on helping the teacher identify professional goals relating to classroom performance, then obtaining valid feedback to assist in reaching those goals. It is often difficult for teachers to separate personal goals from professional goals, and it is especially difficult to separate personal problems from professional ones. Many of the problems administrators identify as deterrents to instructional improvement by their teachers have their basis in personal aspects of the teacher's life—for example, apathy, lack of organization, or emotional instability in the classroom.

It would be convenient if we could exclude personal problems from a discussion of techniques to use in conducting conferences, but they often enter the discussion despite all efforts to stay on a professional level. Most supervisors have had the experience of a teacher crying at some point in a conference. Analyzing behavior is an intensely personal process that often defies a scientific or cold-blooded approach.

Hence, we need ways of dealing with these situations as they arise. It does not seem reasonable for the supervisor to be in tears along with the teacher, yet some expression of sympathy or empathy is in order. If the problems seem to be medical or psychiatric, the course of action is clear: seek help by referring the teacher to an appropriate specialist. Teacher supervisors and school administrators are not competent to make medical diagnoses ("He's an alcoholic" or "She's mentally ill"), and it is definitely not advisable to attempt psychiatric therapy or psychological counseling without the necessary special training and experience. On the other hand, if the problem does not seem to require professional, medical, or psychiatic treatment, a sympathetic listener can often help a person work through a problem.

At the beginning of chapter 10 there is a statement from a university student: "You're the first one around here who has helped me!" This student had sought aid from several advisers in solving a personal problem. One faculty member took the time to listen to the particulars then said, "It seems to me you've identified several possible alternatives. You could drop out of school and work full-time for a while, or you could take a reduced load and work part-time; and you also need to decide whether to get married now or wait." With his own alternatives outlined, the student said, "I see now what I need to do. Thank you."

Client-centered counseling doesn't always work out as quickly or as well, but for a number of reasons it may be an appropriate strategy for the supervisory conference with a teacher. The supervisor does not necessarily know more about teaching kindergarten, French, or physics than the teacher; is probably not aware of as many factors in this particular classroom situation as the teacher; does not expect to spend the rest of the term, year, or career in this teacher's classroom; and will probably rely on the teacher to do most of the follow-up on decisions. It is within the domain of the supervisor to consider what the teacher says about personal problems in the light of how they pertain to peformance in the classroom.

The level of trust the two people have established is a major variable in how helpful a supervisor can be to a teacher with a personal problem that may be interfering with classroom effectiveness. Several factors influence trust building. We tend to trust those who trust us. We tend to trust those whose competence we respect. One way to build a teacher's confidence in our competence as supervisors is to demonstrate our ability to provide useful feedback and to conduct productive conferences.

In some cases a supervisor needs to take full charge of the dealings with certain teachers: selecting what kinds of data will be collected and then analyzing and interpreting that information, drawing conclusions about which goals are being met and which are not, and deciding what needs to be done in the future. At the other extreme, a supervisor may encourage some teachers to set their own goals, select appropriate information to use in assessing the achievement of those goals, and make decisions about future efforts. As pedagogical strategies, these approaches are either didactic or heuristic. How much structure supervisors provide for a conference will depend on their estimate of what kind of atmosphere will provide maximum potential for the growth of a particular teacher.

We have found that when teachers are given a choice of supervisors, some choose one they know to be quite direct whereas others prefer one who tends to be indirect. Teachers who prefer the direct approach may say "I know where she stands" or "He tells it like it is" or "I'm tired of people 'bouncing everything off the wall.'" Those who like an indirect style may say "I feel more comfortable with Mary; she doesn't act like she has all the answers" or "Fred helps me do my own thinking and treats me like a colleague" or "I've had enough of the 'hardsell' approach."

The classroom observer is often cast in a double role: as a colleague helping to improve instruction and as an evaluator. It is sometimes awkward to deal with these two functions simultaneously. For example, to say "I'll devote the first few visits to helping you improve and save the evaluating until later" does not reassure the teacher, nor can the observer forget what has been seen. With teachers who are doing reasonably well, this need not be a problem: "I'm expecting to write a favorable evaluation anyway, so let's concentrate on some areas you'd like to work on" is one approach. Teachers on the borderline deserve to be informed of this fact, but the conference can still be positive and productive. Fair dismissal procedures also require that teachers be given early notice of deficiencies and assistance in attempting to overcome them.

In a few cases, the teacher may be in an "intensive evaluation" situation. (Some districts encourage such a teacher to have an attorney or teacher's organization representative in attendance at any conferences with an evaluator.) Obviously, the tone of the conference will be different in the intensive case. Yet supervisors do not have to turn from Jekyll into Hyde. A skillful parent serves as both counselor and disciplinarian and can do so in a consistent style. Supervisors, too, should be able to fulfill both aspects of their role skillfully.

Dissonance theory provides a rationale for changing teachers' classroom behavior through observational feedback and teacher-centered conferences. The writings of Festinger,[5] Heider,[6] and others supply powerful insights into the dynamics of what Burns expressed in poetic form as the gift of seeing ourselves as others see us. We each have an externally perceived self and an internally perceived self. We develop discomfort when we become aware of a discrepancy between what we believe to be "the real me" and what "the perceived me" seems to be doing—in the eyes of others or in the information collected through systematic observation. For example, a teacher who believes that teachers should smile a lot feels that he smiles a lot; if he views videotapes of himself that show no smiles, he has dissonance. This dissonance can be reduced in several ways, such as:

1. "The videotape is wrong."
2. "It was a bad day, I was nervous."
3. "It isn't really that important to smile so often."

In other words, he can (1) deny the information, (2) reduce the importance of the information, or (3) reduce the importance of the behavior. Another possibility is that he can resolve to make the perceived self more like the "real" or ideal self. That requires changing his behavior.

The goal of supervision for instructional improvement is to get teachers to change their behavior in ways that both they and their supervisors regard as desirable. In some cases only the supervisor (and not the teacher) sees a suggested change as desirable. Now the supervisor experiences dissonance. Among the options for reducing this dissonance are

1. "You'll do it my way, or I'll send you to Siberia."
2. "Let's look at some more data about what is happening."
3. "Let's work on something *you* are concerned about."

In other words, the supervisor may (1) reduce dissonance by forcing compliance from the teacher, or (2) and (3) attempt to achieve consonance through increased understanding of what is on the teacher's mind.

There are times when it is necessary to force teacher compliance to the supervisor's demands—for example, when laws or official school policies are at stake. Most problems that supervisors and teachers work on are not that clear-cut. They concern ways of dealing with students; choosing strategies for teaching certain concepts, skills, or facts; finding alternative ways of managing the many variables in teaching; selecting elements of teaching style that can be modified by the teacher through the use of feedback, practice, and experimentation.

It is unlikely that a teacher can alter a fundamental personality characteristic like dominance, emotional stability, or empathy. Nevertheless, a teacher can learn to use strategies that reduce the tendency to dominate or can develop classroom management techniques that reduce emotional stress. Some outward and visible signs of empathy can be observed, practiced, and incorporated into a teacher's repertoire without resorting to psychiatric therapy or profound religious conversion. Most people who choose teaching as a career have basic qualities that are compatible with the requirements of the job; systematic feedback can inform and convince those who do not.

### Acknowledge and Use What the Person Is Feeling
### (Technique 32)

Rogers[7] reminds us that when a child attempts to do something difficult and says, "I can't," a typical parental response is, "Of course you can!" The response is intended to be positive, but it denies feelings. It might not hurt to say, "It *is* difficult, isn't it, but you'll get it."

Researchers have found that feelings are seldom acknowledged verbally in the classroom.[8] The occurrence in conferences is less well documented, but we suspect that it is unduly limited. When the goal is to change behavior, affective aspects cannot be ignored. The emotions that can be expressed in a conference range from rage to despair, from exhilaration to depression. Clinical supervisors should not ignore the significant emotional content of what teachers are saying any more than they would ignore important cognitive statements.

One way to respond is to describe what you are observing: "You appear to be quite angry about that" or "This seems to make you anxious." Don't be surprised if the teacher's response is "Oh, no, I'm not really angry" or "Who's anxious? I'm not anxious." We tend to deny feelings, as if it were bad to have them, especially in a teaching situation. A psychologist once remarked, "I always knew when my mother was angry at me because she showed it immediately, and I could take that; but my father would wait to 'have a talk with me later,' and that was an agonizing experience." Expressing feelings can be healthy and helpful.

After an expecially satisfying performance before a large class of graduate students, the instructor was told by one student, "I enjoyed seeing that you were relishing the experience." That is a good observation to share. Telling a teacher "You appeared to be enjoying the responses you were getting" or "I shared your apprehension when Dickie volunteered" can have a desirable effect on the tone of the discussion.

## Counseling

For many years we advised supervisors to avoid taking on a counseling role with teachers. We thought it best for supervisors to spend what time they had helping teachers improve their instructional efforts rather than attempting to work on marital, financial, or psychological problems. We felt that the "amateur psychiatrist" would do more harm than good. In the case of serious problems, we still feel this way, but we have modified our position somewhat.

The more we work with supervisors, the more we recognize that it is impossible for them to separate teachers' instructional problems from their personal problems. What is needed is an approach that avoids the pitfalls of inept amateur therapy yet deals honestly with problems expressed by the teacher that have significant impact on classroom performance.

For example, if a teacher says, "I'm spending so much time fighting with my spouse that I just can't get my lessons prepared," the supervisor might do one of several things:

- Threaten to fire the teacher if work does not improve
- Offer advice on how to improve a marriage
- Concentrate on ways of handling schoolwork at school
- Recommend a counselor
- Provide nondirective counseling

Any of the above might work, depending on the situation and the nature of the individuals involved. An objective approach consistent with other techniques in this chapter might be the following:

*Supervisor:* Here are some of the things you've mentioned that would be desirable. Let's indicate them briefly in one column. Here are some things you have identified about the current situation. Let's put them in another column. Now you can add or subtract from either list, but the essential problem is to ask what it takes to get from here to there.

It is conceivable that a conscientious supervisor might perform all the tasks of planning, observing, and giving feedback (as recorded and coded by reliable means) and still not be regarded as helpful by the teacher. We suspect that when this happens, other personality factors or interpersonal dynamics account for the discrepancy. The data we have on what teachers want from a supervisor suggest a fairly open and democratic approach for most teachers. Yet we can use open and democratic procedures to communicate content that is quite structured. Discovery—guided discovery—and didactic teaching are examples of procedures that lie along this continuum.

Rogers,[9] who pioneered client-centered counseling in the 1940s, argues in a recent book for "person-centered" approaches in a wide range of human activities. He contrasts our usual notions of power and control with another view of influence and impact.

## Some Notes on Leadership: Two Extremes

| *Influence and Impact* | *Power and Control* |
|---|---|
| Giving autonomy to persons and groups | Making decisions |
| Freeing people to "do their thing" | Giving orders |
| Expressing own ideas and feelings as one aspect of the group data | Directing subordinates' behavior |
| Facilitating learning | Keeping own ideas and feelings "close to the vest" |
| Stimulating independence in thought and action | Exercising authority over people and organization |
| Accepting the "unacceptable" innovative creations that emerge | Dominating when necessary |
| | Coercing when necessary |
| Delegating, giving full responsibility | Teaching, instructing, advising |
| Offering feedback and receiving it | |

Encouraging and relying on                Evaluating others
   self-evaluation

Finding rewards in the                     Giving rewards; being rewarded
   development and                            by own achievements
   achievements of others

For most teachers, influence and impact are needed from supervisors, not power and control.


## Management

Douglas McGregor's *The Human Side of Enterprise*[10] suggests two approaches to management, theory X and theory Y. They are not opposite poles on a continuum but two different views about work—including teaching and supervising. Theory X applies to traditional management and the assumptions underlying it. Theory Y is based on assumptions derived from research in the social sciences.

Three basic assumptions of theory X are these:

1. The average human being has an inherent dislike of work and will avoid it if possible.
2. Because of this human dislike of work, most people must be coerced, directed, and threatened with punishment to get them to put forth adequate effort toward the achievement of organizational objectives.
3. The average human being prefers to be directed, wishes to avoid responsibility, has relatively little ambition and wants security above all.

McGregor indicates that the "carrot and the stick" theory of motivation fits reasonably well with theory X. External rewards and punishments are the motivators of workers. The consequent direction and control does not recognize intrinsic human motivation.

Theory Y is more humanistic and is based on six assumptions:

1. The expenditure of physical and mental effort in work is as natural as play or rest.
2. External controls and the threat of punishment are not the only means for bringing about effort toward organizational objectives.

Human beings will exercise self-direction and self-control in the service of objectives to which they are committed.

3. Commitment to objectives is a function of the rewards associated with their achievement.

4. The average human being learns, under proper conditions, not only to accept but also to seek responsibility.

5. The capacity to exercise a relatively high degree of imagination, ingenuity, and creativity in the solution of organizational problems is widely, not narrowly, distributed in the population.

6. Under the conditions of modern industrial life, the intellectual potentialities of the average human being are only partially utilized.

McGregor saw these assumptions leading to superior-subordinate relationships in which the subordinate would have greater influence over the activities in his or her own work and also have influence on the superior's actions. Through participatory management, greater creativity and productivity are expected, and also a greater sense of personal accomplishment and satisfaction by the workers. Argyris,[11] Bennis,[12] and Likert[13] cite evidence that a participatory system of management can be more effective than traditional management.

Likert's studies showed that high production can be achieved by managers oriented toward people rather than production. Moreover, these high-production managers were willing to delegate; to allow subordinates to participate in decisions; to be relatively non-punitive; and to use open, two-way communication patterns. High morale and effective planning were also characteristic of these "person-centered" managers. The results may be applied to the supervisory relationship in education as well as to industry.

## Notes

1. Edmund Amidon and Ned Flanders, "Interaction Analysis as a Feedback System," *Interaction Analysis: Theory, Research, and Application*, ed. Edmund Amidon and John Hough (Reading, MA: Addison-Wesley, 1967), pp. 122–124.

2. Arthur Blumberg, *Supervisors and Teachers: A Private Cold War* (Berkeley, CA: McCutchan, 1974).

3. Robert L. Spaulding, "A Coping Analysis Schedule for Educational Settings (CASES)," in *Mirrors for Behavior*, ed. Anita Simon and E. Gil Boyer (Philadelphia: Research for Better Schools, 1967).

4. Everett L. Shostrom, *Man, the Manipulator* (Nashville, TN: Abingdon, 1967).

5. Leon Festinger, *A Theory of Cognitive Dissonance* (Stanford, CA: Stanford University Press, 1968).

6. Fritz Heider, *The Psychology of Interpersonal Relations* (New York: Wiley, 1958).

7. Carl R. Rogers, personal communication, September 1964.

8. Amidon and Hough, *Interaction Analysis*, p. 137.

9. Carl R. Rogers, *Carl Rogers on Personal Power* (New York: Delacorte, 1977), pp. 91–92.

10. Douglas McGregor, *The Human Side of Enterprise* (New York: McGraw-Hill, 1960).

11. Chris Argyris, *Management and Organizational Development* (New York: McGraw-Hill, 1971); idem, *On Organizations of the Future*, (Beverly Hills: Sage, 1973).

12. Warren G. Bennis, *Organizational Development: Its Nature, Origin and Prospects* (Reading, MA: Addison-Wesley, 1967).

13. R. Likert, *New Patterns of Management* (New York: McGraw-Hill, 1961); idem, *The Human Organization* (New York: McGraw-Hill, 1967).

# Unit Exercises

Answers are on page 214.

1. If one attributes the data-collection techniques of unit III to be-havioral psychologists such as B. F. Skinner, the feedback tech-niques of unit IV should be attributed to

    a. J. B. Watson
    b. Sigmund Freud
    c. Carl Rogers
    d. Leon Festinger
    e. David Ausubel

2. From the following, choose the *best* remark for getting the confer-ence down to business:

    a. How do you feel?
    b. How's your family?
    c. You had a good lesson.
    d. Let's take a look at the data I recorded.
    e. You need to be stricter.

3. If a supervisor suspects that a teacher is an alcoholic or is mental-ly ill, it would be best to

    a. confront
    b. refer
    c. prescribe
    d. counsel
    e. ignore

4. Major steps in the feedback process are:

    a. provide data.
    b. analyze data.
    c. interpret what is happening.
    d. make decisions on future actions.
    e. All the above are correct.

5. When a teacher asks a supervisor, "What would *you* do?" the supervisor should:

*a.* refuse to answer.

*b.* describe exactly what to do.

*c.* give several alternatives.

*d.* encourage the teacher to think of several alternatives.

*e.* say, "What would *you* do?"

6. Which of the following fit Carl Rogers's notions of influence and impact (as opposed to power and control)?

*a.* Having teachers make their own tape recordings of lessons.

*b.* Having teachers turn in lesson plans.

*c.* Filing evaluations that are not seen by the teacher.

*d.* Giving merit pay.

*e.* Asking teachers for feedback about supervisory conferences.

7. A behavior that is either direct or indirect is:

*a.* lecturing.

*b.* giving directions.

*c.* giving praise.

*d.* asking questions.

*e.* criticizing.

8. Two behaviors from Spaulding's list that would describe the authors' ideal conference are:

*a.* respond to internal stimuli.

*b.* control.

*c.* transact.

*d.* seek help.

*e.* share.

## Problems

The following problems do not have single correct answers. Answers are on pages 217–19. Your answers may differ from these yet be as good or better.

1. Think of a teacher you have known who had a definite problem with classroom management (student discipline). Then (*a*) list several alternatives this teacher might try. Next (*b*) write a sentence that you would use in suggesting these alternatives to the teacher.

2. Identify a teaching strategy that is not in the list on page 165—

for example, a field trip or committee meetings—and devise a "self-observation" plan a teacher could use to collect data about the lesson.

3. Consider the categories suggested by Spaulding (p. 170). Put them in the first column of a three-column list. In the second column, suggest (with a brief phrase) a common student behavior in the classroom that fits each category. In the third column, identify teacher behaviors in conferences with supervisors that would fit each category. For example:

| Spaulding's list | Student behavior (classroom) | Teacher behavior (conference) |
|---|---|---|
| • | • | • |
| • | • | • |
| • | | |
| Respond to external stimuli | Distracted by another student sharpening pencil | Interrupting conference to deal with a student in the hall |
| • | | |
| • | • | • |
| • | • | • |

# Unit V

# New Roles for Teachers and Principals

## Overview

Throughout the first four units of the book we have emphasized the role of the clinical supervisor in a helping relationship. Unfortunately, what we hear from teachers in many parts of the world (and from supervisors, too) is that this is not the way it is in actual practice, even though most educators who are charged with the responsibility of supervising or evaluating teachers agree that the overwhelming reason for observing, conferring with, or evaluating teachers is to improve instruction. What inhibits us from doing what we should be doing? There are many reasons; we shall address several of them.

In this final unit we propose a way to bring clinical supervision techniques into more frequent use in the schools by modifying the roles that traditionally have been played by teachers and evaluators of teachers.

## Objectives

The objectives of the unit are:

An understanding of the sources of tension in the predominant current arrangements for teacher supervision

An appreciation for what can be possible by rearranging some role
   definitions and job descriptions
Some tangible ways to apply the techniques of clinical supervision
   to the staff development, inservice training activities of school
   districts.

# 12

# New Roles for
# Teachers and Principals[1]

In 1984 the Educational Resources and Information Center (ERIC) Clearinghouse on Educational Management prepared a digest of material on file using the following descriptors: Teacher Supervision, Teacher Effectiveness, Teacher Evaluation, Teacher Improvement, Teacher Recruitment, Screening Tests, Test Validity, Inservice Teacher Education, Staff Development, Teacher Salaries, Elementary-Secondary Education.

The abstract of the investigation's findings is the succinct statement:

> Recent concern for the quality of education has placed pressure on school administrators to assess and upgrade the competency of their teaching staff. No simple formula exists for measuring teacher competency, however, nor are any new methods guaranteed to improve the quality of instruction. Nevertheless, through a combination of clinical supervision, teacher evaluation, and inservice education on one hand and incentive programs coupled with innovative instructional leadership on the other, administrators can increase the likelihood of attracting and retaining competent and devoted professionals in their classrooms.[2]

Few would disagree with the validity of the statement. However, we need to fill in the meaning of the words used. Some of this filling in has been attended to in other units—what clinical supervision is and how it can be conducted, for example. Teacher evaluation was considered in chapter 3. Inservice education and incentive programs are topics for other books. We do believe that the techniques of clinical supervision should be made available (through inservice education) to many teachers as well as to principals and other administrators. Career ladders for teachers should recognize these skills as prerequisite for various new roles within instructional leadership.

The focus of this chapter is on some new roles that are emerging within the domain of instructional leadership.

## Sources of Tension

Supervisors of inservice teachers may have a number of other responsibilities: teaching, administration, management, public relations, curriculum, budget, student discipline, health, safety, nutrition, and many more. As one of our administrator colleagues pointed out, when confronted with the fact that school administrators seem more concerned with budgets than supervision, "If you want to get fired, making a mistake in the budget is much quicker than making an omission in supervision." This is still true. However, there is a clear call from those who pay for education asking for an emphasis on improving instruction and an insistence on accountability for those who provide it. The organizations that represent teachers are also recognizing this need. They are saying, "Let's evaluate teachers regularly. If they need help, let's provide it. If they are still unable (or unwilling) to improve, let's dismiss them and replace them."

To carry out the ultimate purpose of clinical supervision (the improvement of instruction), we need some new roles. One might be the principal who has someone else to do public relations, nutrition, inoculation, budgets, discipline. Another might be the principal of a small school who also teaches, coaches, and otherwise does almost everything to provide excellence to the patrons of a rural, or isolated, school. On the other hand, one might be a department head in a large school in a major city.

What are these roles that must be filled? Who can fill them? It seems to depend on the situation. In the western provinces of Canada, it may be a principal who belongs to the same professional association as the teachers he or she supervises. In the Middle East, it may be a "supervisor" or "inspector." On the West Coast of the United States, it may be a "mentor teacher," "master teacher," or "instructional leader."

We have concluded, after discussions with and surveys of many school people in several states, provinces, and countries, that for the typical school principal (and other building administrators if it is a big school) two observations per teacher per year would represent a substantial increase over what is currently happening. There are, of course, notable exceptions. The Rand study[3] of exemplary programs identified several districts where a high priority is placed on regular and frequent observation of instruction by observers whose training and experience qualify them to be instructional leaders.

If these leaders are principals or other administrators, they must have the time—and use it—to be in classrooms making objective and relevant observations. If the observers are teachers, then they need the time and the skills to carry out the planning, recording, and feedback phases of the clinical supervision cycle. Two cycles per year are not enough to generate and sustain substantial changes in teaching behavior. Six or eight cycles would be more realistic. If the building administrator is making two of these for formal (summative) evaluation purposes, then four or more could be made by colleagues for developmental (formative) purposes.

The immediate reaction to such a plan is concern for its cost. If every teacher were willing to devote one hour per month either to observing and conferring with others (if qualified) or to replacing one who is qualified, most schools could accommodate this within their schedules. In return for this "donated" time, each teacher would receive the benefits of several observations and conferences with a qualified colleague who would be serving as a constructively critical friend. Additional time, in the form of paid substitutes, can be provided by the school board.

We shall pursue these new roles simultaneously—a new role for principals, which includes more supervision and consequently less of something else, and a new role for teachers as collegial observers and as givers and receivers of feedback with colleagues.

## A Persistent Problem

One of the most persistent problems in supervision is the dilemma between (1) evaluating a teacher in order to make decisions about retention, promotion, and tenure, or (2) working with the teacher as a friendly critic or colleague to help develop skills the teacher wants to use and to expand the repertoire of strategies that can be employed.

We have struggled for many years with the tension that results

from these different purposes for observation, feedback, goal setting, planning, and the other activities of clinical supervision. In
some respects the two outcomes, evaluation and help, are compatible. Many jobs combine the two functions. For example, the vice
principal of a school may be in charge of student counseling and
discipline. Of course, students who are called to the office may be
apprehensive about whether they will receive therapy or be ex-
pelled. Parents are both evaluators and disciplinarians and at the same
time supervisors and counselors. Some parents, and some administrators, handle this double-agent role gracefully and convincingly
(though we never did believe "This is going to hurt me more than
you").

Supervising and evaluating teachers demands an especially delicate balance. Effective supervision requires a high level of trust.
Teachers often regard any evaluation that is less than laudatory as
an attack on their character. To evaluate them as teachers is to
evaluate them as persons. It is difficult to trust someone who is (in
your mind) slandering and defaming your heart and soul.

Another way to reconcile the tension between supervision and
evaluation is to agree that both are for the same ultimate purpose—
the improvement of instruction. All instructors can improve; some
have only growth needs; some also have deficiency needs; some
have intensive needs; a few have desperate needs.

## Our Position

Despite the foregoing rationales for a single role, our position in this
final unit is that it would be best to separate the role of clinical
supervisor or helpful colleague from the role of evaluator. We may
label the functions of the former as "formative" and the latter as
"summative."

An implication of this separation is that others besides the evaluator will plan with and observe teachers and provide feedback
strictly for the purpose of improvement. The evaluator's observations will be for the purpose of writing a formal, summative
assessment of the teacher. Data or other documentation from the
formative phase will only be used at the request of the teacher.

Another implication of separating the two functions is that we
shall have to adapt to some new roles in many schools. These
schools are accustomed to having administrators as supervisors

and evaluators. Our formative friends would be colleagues—other teachers, department heads, team leaders, "mentors"—not line administrators.

A third implication is that these collegial observers need certain skills and understanding in order to fulfill their new roles effectively. Many of the skills (or techniques) that an effective collegial observer needs are the same as those of a clinical supervisor which have been described in other chapters. Depending on the role that is developed in various situations, the instructional leader who is not an administrator may need additional skills and training. We shall explore some of these possibilities in this chapter.

A fourth implication of creating new roles for teachers is that the role of the administrator will need to change with, adapt to, and complement the new roles that teachers will play. We shall consider some new roles that teachers will play. We shall also consider some new roles that principals or other administrators might play.

## New Roles for Teachers

We have mentioned two out of three topics that have received increased attention in recent years: teacher evaluation, teacher supervision, and teacher effectiveness. Are these all part of the same thing? Are they related in some systematic way? Are they separate and immiscible?

One way to relate them is to think in terms of outputs, that is, ends and means. The product of teacher evaluation is decisions about retention, promotion, or dismissal. The product of teacher supervision should be improved teaching. The result of teacher effectiveness is student learning. These observations might lead us to conclude that our three topics are quite different and distinct.

Another approach would be to ask who works with these concepts. The school principal is usually expected to evaluate teachers, supervise them, and help them to be more effective. Viewed from this perspective, the three concepts all fit into a single role. Could they be separated into different roles? Could colleagues take responsibility for "supervising" (that is, observing and giving feedback to) each other? Could teacher organizations take the lead in "quality control" by organizing support groups or other staff development activities? Can teachers be evaluated by others besides school administrators?

With these questions in mind, let us step back and view the topics from a historical perspective. Education as a profession has tended to move from an "inspector" model of employee monitoring to a more democratic, collaborative one. The participation of the teacher in setting goals for self-improvement, choosing sources of feedback, and making decisions about desirable changes has received increased attention over the years. The responses to surveys of teachers and supervisors in several countries have indicated that this is the kind of supervision teachers (and many supervisors) are seeking.

The most available source of expertise is teachers themselves: to analyze their own teaching on the basis of objective data, to observe in others' classrooms and record data teachers cannot record themselves, to help one another analyze these data and make decisions about alternative strategies. Some new roles for teachers can allow them to do these things without becoming evaluators. In our scenario the principal (or other responsible administrator) will still do the formal evaluation. Evaluators need the skills and techniques of clinical supervision as well, but first we are considering what part teachers can, and should, play.

Several forces are pushing us to create new roles in the schools for instructional leaders. One is the increased role conflict felt by building principals who are expected to be hard-nosed evaluators of teachers and also kindly, sympathetic, helpful supervisors of instruction. Another pressure comes from task forces and special commissions who recommend career ladders for teachers along with other incentives and rewards to stimulate and improve the performance of the schools.

Some momentum is developing within the profession through teachers' organizations that are promoting more careful screening at entry levels, more support and better staff development opportunities for inservice teachers, and better on-the-job supervision. Tougher teacher evaluation laws emphasize the need for better programs of assistance for teachers with serious deficiencies and, when necessary, fair dismissal procedures.[4]

Perhaps the most important reason to look for alternative sources of instructional leadership is that traditional arrangements are, in many cases, not getting the job done adequately. The functions of supervision are not being carried out well in many schools. Teachers are not being observed regularly or systematically, nor are they being provided with useful feedback that they can use to improve instruction or increase effectiveness. Some reasons why the functions of instructional leadership are not being performed well are:

- lack of time
- lack of knowledge of a range of observational techniques by supervisors and other observers
- lack of understanding of a variety of instructional strategies by teachers and supervisors
- lack of interpersonal skills used by observers in providing feedback to teachers

If others besides the principal are to take part in supervision and improvement of instruction, then we first need to consider what roles they will play. We shall refer to these roles by a single label, *instructional leader.*

Supervision and evaluation are the two activities that are most important to the instructional leader in dealing with teachers. Related topics are recruitment, selection, staff development, inservice training, assignment, dismissal, and due process. Because supervision of teachers is moving away from the role of an inspector toward the role of a friendly critic or collegial observer, we shall emphasize, as appropriate for teacher colleagues, what a friendly critic (or critical friend) should do. Suitable activities would include the observation/feedback activities of supervision that have been described in other units and the setting of teacher goals by the teacher and an instructional leader or colleague (chapter 4). They would not include formal report writing or other procedures that are associated with summative evaluation.

### Behaviors of the Instructional Leader

What might we expect to see an instructional leader doing?

*Interacting with Teachers.* This might be before or after an individual observation, in informal conversation, or in a group meeting. Leadership cannot take place in isolation from the instructors.

*Planning, Assessing, and Modifying the Curriculum.* Much of this activity will take place in conjunction with others. Surveying materials will require individual activity.

*Being in the Classroom.* Observing students, teachers, and activities is often neglected by principals, and the reason is usually lack of time.

*Placing High Priority on Instructional Leadership Responsibilities.* To translate this statement into observable behavior, consider the following: Given the choice among several options, which will most school people choose—chasing a dog from the playground, taking a phone call from a parent, taking a phone call from the superintendent, or keeping an appointment with a teacher for a postobservation conference? Those who analyze time management point to two forces governing such decisions—which activities have the highest "payoff" and which we like to do. If educators believe that instructional leadership activities, such as meeting with a teacher to discuss an observation, are both potent and enjoyable, then there is a chance that priorities can be rearranged from what they now appear to be.

*Keeping Informed about Forces Affecting Instruction.* School leaders should know about research on how the brain functions and how computers can be applied to school programs. Besides knowing about pertinent research and new technology, instructional leaders have a companion responsibility to share this information with other teachers. Many teachers are unaware of the existence of different models of teaching besides the one(s) they are using, or of systematic classroom observation techniques that might help them analyze and improve their own teaching.

*Organizing for Instructional Improvement.* Many of the meetings teachers attend deal with procedural and bureaucratic matters. As a contrast, consider department meetings in a secondary school or unit meetings in an elementary school where faculty members regularly view excerpts from videotapes made in their classrooms on a revolving basis so that they can analyze and discuss the content, methodology, and techniques of their teaching as a substantial part of the meeting. If this were to become a widespread practice, we should see some striking improvements.

*Being an Advocate for Teachers.* Helping a teacher get a tape recorder for use in the classroom is one example of advocacy; helping to develop appropriate activities is another. Finding materials, equipment, ideas, and printed articles that teachers might use is an explicit means for a leader to show that he or she is an advocate, not a watchdog or inspector. Going to bat for a teacher who is involved in a controversy is another example of advocacy.

*Diagnosing Learning Problems.* The mainstreaming law has caused school leaders to design Individual Educational Plans (IEPs) for students with handicaps. Teachers and principals have always given individual attention to the students who have the biggest (or most obvious) problems, be they physical, emotional, or attitudinal. Perhaps the design of an IEP with an instructional leader, a teacher, counselor, and parent working cooperatively can be thought of as a model for dealing with all students, not just the handicapped. We have seen tension develop in schools over the problem students. A cooperative mode can make the leader a more intimate part of the instructional team. It also provides a support group for the teachers who have the most immediate concerns with specific students.

*Selecting Instructional Activities.* We usually think of the teacher as the person who selects activities. The leadership may have a strong hand (often applied subtly) in this process. Some schools have lots of field trips; others don't. The leader's attitude toward these may have been instrumental. Some schools have lots of problem-solving activities, role-playing, group activities; others don't. The philosophy of the leadership is probably reflected in this situation.

*Selecting Instructional Materials.* Leadership can be expressed in which maps, supplementary reading materials, things to be manipulated by students, and other devices are purchased. These decisions also influence what may happen in instruction. When censorship becomes an issue, the leadership function sharpens. The principal of the Mark Twain School who agreed that *Huckleberry Finn* should be removed from the library was in an interesting bind.

*Communicating with the Community.* Football teams, marching bands, and other performing groups communicate parts of the school's program to the public. The instructional program is often not so well shared. A function of leadership is to find ways to let the patrons know about the academic as well as the extracurricular programs.

*Communicating with Students.* One principal of a successful (award-winning) high school sometimes sings in the choir, plays in the band, and takes part in various other organizations and activities. The message (stronger than words) is "I approve of what you are doing; it's important." When commended for this behavior, he responded, "I wish I knew how to reach the guys smoking in the parking lot better." It would be interesting to analyze the content of educators' informal conversations with students over a period of time and then speculate as to their impact on the instructional program.

In 1977 Jo Ann Mazzarella summarized the principal's role as instructional leader in a publication of the ERIC Clearinghouse on Educational Management and the Association of California School Administrators.[5] The point was made that the role is constantly changing; however, a number of the observations made at that time can still be made today. Some of the things that principals or others can do as leaders of the instructional program are as follows:

*Principals*

- orient faculty to new teaching techniques
- make classroom visits, evaluate,* give feedback
- involve parents, teachers, counselors, and administrators in developing the grading system
- supervise the testing program
- schedule time for teachers to discuss their concerns
- visit meetings of teams and departments
- devote faculty meetings to what is happening in instructional areas
- relate needs of students to school system goals and legal requirements
- supervise inservice education
- provide liaison between the schools and the community
- manage change
- allow discussions directed toward innovations
- provide adequate time and support for innovations
- provide constant evaluation of the entire school*
- coordinate the efforts of unit leaders*

### Role as Staff Developer

Staff development is a topic related to the supervision and evaluation of teachers. The instructional leader's responsibility for promoting the professional development of the teaching staff is so important for the school's success as to warrant fuller discussion.

Writing in 1981 about the principal as staff developer, Roland Barth emphasized the need for interacting with teachers in ways that encourage growth rather than merely force compliance.[6] He identified three groups of teachers:

1. Teachers who are unable and unwilling to examine their teaching practice critically and unable to have other adults—teachers, principals, parents—examine what and how they are teaching.
2. Teachers who are quite able and willing to scrutinize continually and reflect upon what they do and make use of their insights to effect periodic changes.
3. Teachers, few in number, who are able and willing to scrutinize their practice critically *and* who are quite able and willing, even desirous, of others having access to what they do.

---

*These functions should be performed by line administrators; the others can be carried out by collegial leaders.

We agree with Barth that one of the major tasks of the instructional leader (or staff developer) is to move teachers from 1 to 3. Of course, teachers examine themselves and respond to feedback from others in more than three ways, but these three are certainly bench marks along the continuum.

A supervisor of teachers has to deal with the full range of personality types. These range from aggressive to passive, from authoritarian to laissez-faire, from any extreme to its opposite. We need instructional leaders who understand these variations in personality types. For example, inflexible teachers will not respond well to hints; hypersensitive teachers will not react in a healthy way to harsh criticism. Linear teachers may not be tolerant of digressions; heuristic teachers may scorn dogma.

### Leading a Group of Teachers

We have been considering a supervisor (or other leader) working with individual teachers. In addition, group techniques are needed. Some of the qualities needed to lead a group of teachers are the same ones teachers need to lead a group of students. Let us take a closer look at several of these.

*Clarity.*   It has been shown that the clarity of the teacher's communication is related to student achievement. No doubt the instructional leader's clarity is related to teacher achievement. If what the leader expects is not clear, it is unlikely to happen. When a group is attempting to solve a problem, the ability to clarify what the problem is can be most useful. Being able to clarify what others are saying can also be of great help to the group.

*Enthusiasm.*   Enthusiasm is essential to the leader of a group. We would advocate an even stronger word, *surgence*. To be "up" for the occasion and to be excited about the people involved and the content of the discussion are examples of "surgent" behavior. Its opposite is apathy, one of the symptoms of which is "burnout."

*Variety.*   A variety of strategies, activities, and goals can be as refreshing to a group of teachers as to a class of students. The leader who avoids monotony by varying the approach from meeting to meeting will have less trouble keeping the group engaged in the topic at hand, which is the next quality.

*Keeping the Group on Task.*   Sticking to business has been the strongest variable associated with student achievement in recent research that has tried to link teacher behaviors to student outcomes. Task involvement would seem equally important to the instructional leader working with a group of teachers in a problem-solving, staff development or curriculum development process.

*Indirect Behaviors.*   Though there are many other useful characteristics of group leadership, dealing with feelings as well as ideas, acknowledging and praising others' ideas, and using others' ideas are all behaviors that can be put to good use. Lecturing, giving directions, and criticizing will also be used when appropriate. The leader of a group of teachers will usually get further with the former than with the latter.

The relationship between the last two categories deserves special attention. The balance between structure or task orientation and human relations is a delicate one. A leader with a high task/low relations emphasis will be perceived as authoritarian and will tend to tell the group what to do. One who is high on task and also high on relations will tend to sell them on his or her ideas (especially if he or she is surgent). One who places low emphasis on structure but is high on relations will tend to participate with the group. Finally, one with low emphasis on both task and relations will tend to delegate. Hersey, Blanchard, and others have written at some length about these relationships.[7] An effective leader should be able to play the role of teller, seller, participator, or delegator depending on the situation. The predominant situation for collegial instructional leaders would seem to call for a participator (low structure/high relations).

In general, what we have found in our surveys is that teachers want an instructional leader who will meet with them individually, discuss *their* concerns, help select appropriate ways to collect data from observation and other means, cooperatively analyze the data, and consider alternatives. They want a colleague who is skilled at observation, knowledgeable about teaching, and supportive.

Broudy has described three fundamental kinds of teaching in "Didactics, Heuristics, and Philetics."[8] The third approach comes close to what teachers seem to be seeking. It is a mentor model characterized by positive regard, individualized guidance, and strong dependence on the nature of the relationship: Horace Mann at one end of the log and me at the other.

Few school leaders would deny the reasonableness of these teacher preferences. The kind of instructional leadership teachers say they prefer is also what a broad range of research findings say they should be receiving. Studies of "coaching" with teachers, for example, have underlined the need for consistent follow-up by trainers or supervisors on the practice of new skills.

Despite general agreement on what should be the ideal state of supervisory practice, it has not yet become reality except in isolated instances. What stands in the way? The chief obstacle may well be the traditional model whereby supervision and evaluation are exercised by only one person in the school: the principal. Several limitations on the principal's role serve to stifle the capacity to realize the full supervisory potential: lack of time, lack of specific training and expertise in the techniques of supervision, and the tension caused by the fact that the principal is usually the evaluator as well as the supervisor of teachers.

### New Role Definitions

Instructional leadership can be separated into four major categories—curriculum development, supervision, teacher evaluation, and management. Teacher evaluation and supervision are often treated together as two parts of the same process. However, the requirements of evaluation often detract from the potential effectiveness of supervision. The apprehension and defensiveness that are frequently associated with supervision are intensified by formal evaluation. Moreover, the demands of management leave little time for supervision and promote a perspective that may not be sensitive to the central concerns of instruction.

Perhaps we need some new role definitions that permit someone to work with teachers in a way that will encourage them to reach their potential without the threat and apprehension that usually accompany supervision and evaluation. We shall try several scenarios that break up the current combination of manager/evaluator/supervisor/adviser. That combination may be inappropriate to the purposes of instructional leadership.

For our first scenario, let's call our teacher "Cinderella," for she has an adviser who is a fairy godmother whom we shall call "Wanda." Wanda tends to appear "before the fact" rather than after; that is, she gives encouragement and confidence so that Cinderella can do what she wants to do, despite the obstacles. If Cindy wants to try role-playing, simulation, or games to reach an instructional goal, Wanda is up for it! Furthermore, she'll help get Cindy out of trouble—at midnight! Many of us would have welcomed a Wanda at some point in our teaching career when we might have ventured out, but didn't.

We'll call another teacher "Arthur." His supervisor is "Merlin," who is a wizard. Merlin's ideas about what activities will work and which materials are appropriate are incredible. Whereas Wanda's contributions were affective (they gave us the courage to go ahead with what we thought would work), Merlin's are cognitive (they suggest approaches we would not have thought of).

Let's call another teacher "Prince." His adviser is a supervisor known as "Machiavelli." Mac is a process person. He's had training and experience in interpersonal relations and organizational development. He has a feel for how folks will respond to situations. His analysis of what's going on in a discussion is perceptive and useful. His notions about how one can facilitate learning are helpful to a teacher who wants to give "inside help" to students.

Polya distinguishes "inside help" (that which aids students to solve problems using their own powers) from "outside help" (that which makes use of the teacher's prowess).[9] Mac has some ambiguity about this. Taking satisfaction in prowess to give "inside help" rather than "outside help" requires an unusual ego. One must be comfortable with oneself to do so.

Another teacher we shall call "Em Peror." Em's advisers overlook the obvious fact that his clothes are not merely fine but nonexistent. Going before our clients naked on the advice of our counselors is still embarrassing. The difference between Em's advisers and Wanda is that they are sycophants, whereas she only encourages that which is feasible.

Supervisors of teachers may not readily identify with Em's advisers, but flattery can be overdone in dealing with teachers as well as with emperors. Uncritical praise can produce undesirable results; positive reinforcement is best applied to specific, desirable behavior that we wish to encourage. We tend to think of factory foremen as overemphasizing the negative, but educators who are lavish with undeserved praise may be as much at fault.

Another teacher might be called "Othello." His supervisor is "Iago." One finds evidence in teacher dismissal hearings of supervisors who are almost as devious as the treacherous Iago in the "bum steers" they give to teachers who are in need of sincere help, not betrayal.

We could go on with literary and historical allusions; Boswell makes an interesting model as an observer and giver of feedback. However, it may be more useful to construct some general categories that can contain these various types.

*Counselor.*  Many supervisors choose the role of counselor. Provided that personal counsel is not given at the expense of feedback on teaching, it can be a helpful adjunct. The line between teaching concerns and personal problems is often a fine one.

*Coach.* The term "coach" connotes a range of activities that may be appropriate to instructional leadership. The emphasis on explicit, focused feedback based on expert observation of performance is certainly appropriate. Persistent and repeated supervised practice is a feature of coaching that is often missing in the development of teaching skills. Our colleagues who are studying the coaching process in relation to teachers see transfer of training—that is, the continued application of newly learned skills—as the weakest link in most preservice and inservice teacher training efforts.

*Inspector.* A role that has been associated with supervision in the past and is still used as an official title in some parts of the world is that of inspector. Quality control is a function of supervision or instructional leadership, but it can be achieved without the pejorative overtones we tend to associate with "inspection."

*Mentor.* Broudy uses the label "mentor" in association with a form of teaching he called "Philetic" (based on love and emphasizing a one-to-one relationship as opposed to Didactic or Heuristic teaching). The notion of a mentor fits our concept of an ideal supervisor.

*Master.* Like "boss" and "overseer," "master" seems to belong to a bygone era when Theory X was in common use.[10]

The new roles have several advantages in addition to the likelihood that teachers will respond more positively to a new kind of leadership. They can provide a career ladder for teachers who do not wish to become administrators yet do wish to advance in the profession. They can provide a means for teacher organizations to play a positive role in the improvement of competence within the profession.

If successfully implemented, such a program could be cost-beneficial. Two examples may illustrate the point. In one case litigation brought by a teacher cost nearly a quarter of a million dollars in attorney fees alone; in another a reinstated teacher became a nonproductive liability that, over the years, may have cost a half million dollars in salary, administrative time, legal fees, and the like. If these cases had been worked out cooperatively by the school districts and teacher organizations rather than as labor/management confrontations, those same funds could have bought a lot of inservice training or released time for collegial supervision. Effective collegial leadership would serve as a preventive in such cases.

Because principals have so many roles to fill and severe limitations on their capacity to carry out those roles, is it unreasonable to expect that they might share some of their responsibilities with other personnel? In instructional matters, particularly, others can share the leadership role. Department heads in high schools have traditionally been responsible for concerns that were specific to the subject matter. Elementary schools that are organized into units often have team leaders for each of the units.

In large schools the supervision and evaluation responsibilities often are shared with other administrators. Many of the management functions can also be delegated. The resource that is least often drawn upon is teachers, who can provide observations, feedback, psychological support, and expert analysis for their colleagues.

### Department Heads

Department heads in secondary schools have the advantage of being subject-matter specialists in their field. Thus they avoid the skepticism principals often receive—"How can a former math teacher supervise and evaluate a foreign language teacher?" Department heads are also concerned about, and in immediate contact with, the curriculum in their department. However, they have often shied away from assuming responsibilities for supervising teachers or making major decisions about the curriculum. A redefinition of the role and provision for revelant training are needed to make department heads true instructional leaders.

What might a department head hope to accomplish by taking on a new role as instructional leader? To answer the question, let's imagine a possible case. Pat is head of a high school mathematics department and receives a stipend plus a free period each day for carrying out the tasks of the assignment. Pat has had training and experience in using the skills of observing and analyzing teaching and giving feedback to the seven department members. Some of them have similar skills, so sometimes Pat takes their classes while they observe a colleague. At least ten observations are made each month so each teacher (including Pat) has six to eight per year. These are regarded as formative by the teachers, and they choose goals to work on that are consistent with their growth needs and concerns.

In addition to the personal growth that these teachers achieve, there are some spinoffs. Because they observe one another's classes, there is a coherence to the program. They know what others are doing and can articulate sequences of courses and activities. They have a mutual sense of psychological and professional support. They share teaching ideas, and when curriculum is being modified, they analyze the effects at a concrete level. They have overcome their apprehension about videotaping their own teaching for self-analysis. The students are also accustomed to having observers and recorders in the room. One can see the effects of Pat's leadership (and the cooperation of colleagues) in morale, school climate, student achievement, and job satisfaction.

If department heads are to assume greater responsibility as instructional leaders, several other changes may need to occur. There should be prerequisite training in supervision skills and curriculum matters. Most incumbents will need more time for classroom visits than they now have. There also should be a proportionate increase in authority to accompany any increase in responsibility. For example, the department head might have the authority to change teaching assignments, allocate materials, modify curriculum, establish testing programs. Writing formal evaluations of their fellow teachers would place the same strain on the trust relationship that has been mentioned earlier; hence we would not recommend it.

### Teaching Colleagues

Experiments with team teaching may not have proved that it increased achievement by students, but they did show that teachers can benefit from working closely with colleagues. In a team, teachers vicariously pick up teaching techniques from one another and are exposed to an expanded repertoire of strategies. If teachers were trained in systematic observation procedures, they would be the ideal persons to provide feedback to one another. They and their professional organizations are opposed to becoming evaluators of other teachers, but they are usually enthusiastic when given responsibilities for staff devleopment.

To make use of the talents and skills of teachers, some adjustments need to be made to allow and encourage them to observe in one another's classrooms and to have time to meet and discuss what they have observed. Collegial supervision also has implications for inservice training: teachers must develop the skills of systematic observations and helpful feedback.

Creating instructional leadership roles for teachers requires some imagination. For one thing, teachers in this role will need a label or title. We also need to define the functions. For example, we might call them *master teachers* and place them in charge of student teachers and teacher aides in addition to setting a minimum number of classroom observations and conferences with each of several other teachers. Another area of special concern could be new teachers. There are other possible functions in connection with curriculum, counseling, testing, and the like. California has begun to use "mentor teachers" to perform these functions.

### Other Sources of Instructional Leadership

*Other Administrators.*   Vice principals can perform any of the functions we have discussed. Administrators in the central offices of larger school districts often have skills for working with teachers and could benefit from spending time in the schools, but they tend to become isolated and desk-bound. Subject-matter supervisors for large school districts may visit classrooms, give demonstration lessons, choose or recommend curriculum materials, provide inservice training, and in other ways interact directly with teachers about the instructional program.

*Students.*   Students can supply useful data for the feedback process. Questionnaires can be used to tap their perceptions, and interviews with them can provide a rich source of information. Students can also operate videotape cameras for teachers who are undertaking self-analysis.

*Self-analysis.*   This technique has not had the amount of use that it deserves. Parsons, in the 1960s, developed guides that can be used to analyze one's own videotapes.[11] Minicourses, which were self-instructional units for teachers who wanted to develop new skills, used self-analysis of videotapes guided by a teacher's handbook as the feedback phase of a demonstration-practice strategy. They were very successful in helping teachers to change their classroom behavior.

### Conclusion

Creating new roles for teachers requires support at the policy level, administrative cooperation, special training, and some hard work on the part of the teachers. Whatever these roles are called and however they are implemented, the techniques of clinical supervision will be essential.

## Role of the Principal

The courts, arbitrators, and hearing panels regard the principal as the person most responsible for making judgments in respect to the evaluation of teachers. In some jurisdictions the superintendent is responsible by law or regulation, but may delegate the responsibility to others, usually principals. Given this responsibility, the principal has a difficult task being also a clinical supervisor in the collegial, constructively critical mode we have advocated. We know some principals who are able to do so and maintain a high level of trust and mutual respect with their teachers. Their competence in the techniques of clinical supervision is a major source of this respect and trust. Despite the encouragement that such principals provide, the majority of teachers do not feel that they are getting the kind of supervision they want and need.

Our response to the existing situation is twofold. First, we need more principals who are trained and experienced in systematic observation and feedback techniques. When they have become skilled, their evaluation activities can provide useful information for the improvement of instruction. These evaluation activities can be a part of instructional leadership rather than empty ritual. Second, the principal needs to share the instructional leadership of the school with teachers and others who are taking on new roles in the instructional program.

There will be a new role for the principal to play in managing the logistics to make collegial observation and analysis possible. Another role may be to provide inservice training or staff development activities that enable teachers to develop the skills necessary to become effective colleagues in a program that uses peer observation and analysis. Another role for the principal will be to work with probationary teachers (those who have not attained tenure) or with teachers who would prefer not to work with peers.

In addition to the new roles, the principal will still have the old role of summative evaluator. In most districts this responsibility will require (or imply) at least two observations in a year in which a teacher is being formally evaluated. For many schools that many observations will represent a quantum leap. Our information from several parts of the world (about how often teachers are observed by their evaluators) substantiates our rash claim that most teachers are rarely observed, and when they are, the feedback from the observer is not regarded as helpful. Hence, being in the classroom as a skilled observer for either formative or summative purposes represents a new role for many principals.[12]

One role we do not advocate for a principal is as a member of the committee administering a program of assistance for a teacher who is on notice if that teacher was put on notice by the principal in question. There is often a question of bias or personal conflict in such cases, and it is best to have a "neutral" administrator on the committee as we suggested in chapter 3.

A role that is necessary is to monitor and encourage the peer observation process. Even though teachers who have participated in such programs are enthusiastic about their beneficial effects, the number of competing events in a school calendar can intrude and diminish the effectiveness of the process (which needs to be consistently pursued).

### Role Analogies for Clarifying the Supervisory Role

We have identified some literary archetypes that apply to supervisory roles and will now assign them some categorical names. Cinderalla's fairy godmother, Wanda, was playing the part of a *mentor*, a kindly and often indulgent role taken by one, usually older, in shaping the career of a protégé. Merlin (at King Arthur's court) played the role of a *maestro*, or master of an art, who shares his knowledge and cunning with other, appreciative persons. Machiavelli might be called a *coach* today—one who observes closely the performance of others over time and gives advice for improvement. Iago was a *counselor* to Othello, albeit not a benign one.

The principal as instructional leader may play any or all of these roles, but will tend to emphasize one over the others. Therefore, let us look at some of the dangers inherent in each. The mentor can work with only a limited number of protégés, whereas the school principal has a whole building full. To be a maestro in the symphony of learning that we conduct in schools requires being a master of many arts. Moreover, the principal is expected to be an impresario as well.

The coaching metaphor has been strongly advocated recently,[13] and we tend to agree that this model fits the schools. One who wants to see teachers develop and improve continuously must observe carefully over time, understand and use a range of strategies, and employ techniques that communicate the knowledge of strategies and the information from observation to the teachers.

The counselor role is helpful up to a point; becoming involved in the teacher's nonprofessional, personal affairs may be beyond the scope of an instructional leader.

### The Principal as Coach

Because we have expressed a preference for the coaching role, let us pursue it a bit further. Can you imagine an Olympic coach merely saying to an athlete, "That was pretty good, but I know you can do better"? No, we expect to hear, "You're taking your eye off the target at the last instant. Let's look at the videotapes I made and compare them with those of your best performance." We would also be surprised to hear such a coach say that he or she would be around to watch two or three times during the year and then write a final report in the spring. We expect the coaching to be continuous and frequent, even after the athlete achieves world status.

How, then, shall we translate the coaching analogy into the real work of the principal? It seems that in a school of appreciable size (30 or more teachers) the head coach needs some assistants. These need not be additional administrators, but may be other teachers who, during free periods or released time, can observe and meet with teachers who are working to achieve growth needs or to overcome deficiency needs.

### Alternative Arrangements

For a number of years we have pondered the plight of the typical principal who must play the double role of supervisor and evaluator. We have tried to say and write things that would help make the situation more tolerable. Probably the best solution to this dilemma is to train teachers to observe one another and to provide feedback for formative purposes as part of the staff development program. Formal evaluation for summative purposes—retention decisions, promotion, tenure—would still be the responsibility of administrators.

Another possibility is to use one set of administrators as supervisors and another as evaluators. Department heads in secondary schools would also be natural choices for the supervisory role. The data from supervisor observations would not be used for evaluation unless the teacher requested it.

Another alternative is peer evaluation. Teachers, beyond just helping each other to improve, can actually write formal, summative evaluations on one another. This has been done successfully at the junior college level, but is unlikely to gain acceptance at the elementary and secondary levels. Teacher organizations appear to be opposed to having their members engage in evaluating one another. The prevalence of collective bargaining and also legal distinctions between supervisors and teachers affect who can evaluate.

As we expand our notions of instructional leadership to include others besides the building principal, various divisions of responsibility will take place. For the time being, evaluation will continue to be the responsibility of the principal in most cases, but there will be increasing pressure to provide supervision for instructional improvement, perhaps using other kinds of leadership roles.

## Conclusion

We have emphasized the role of the instructional leader as a special kind of clinical supervisor. The role may be shared by a principal with others. Matters such as curriculum guidance and assistance with student discipline are also important. Whoever is the instructional leader, direct involvement through classroom observation and interaction with teachers cannot be neglected. Our analogies all contain this element of direct involvement: the mentor, the maestro, the coach, and the counselor.

Our experience with principals in the field suggests that they often neglect this role; lack of time is usually the reason. There are other reasons. Interacting with teachers about their teaching can be a sticky business. The teachers are often defensive and resentful, and principals often lack skill and training in the prerequisites for a good relationship.

These prerequisites are as follows: a repertoire of observational skills and recording techniques, a working knowledge of a range of instructional strategies, a set of interpersonal communication skills, and feedback strategies to use in conferences with teachers. A number of these techniques have been discussed in the preceding chapters. Our research indicates that these techniques are what teachers are looking for but in many cases are not getting.

The studies of effective schools have placed great importance on the effectiveness of the principal. The principal's effectiveness depends, in large part, on instructional leadership. This leadership can be shared with others.

## Training and Practice

In order to have the skills ("techniques," we have called them) necessary to carry out the functions of these new roles, principals and teachers need training and practice. We have found that 20 to 30 hours of instruction plus an equal amount of practice (at least ten observations using different techniques, including at least five full cycles with planning before and feedback after) should be adequate.

It is desirable to have both teachers and administrators in such a class. If the training is undertaken within a school system, then teachers' apprehensions are allayed when they learn what the purposes are and what the effects can be. Administrators with only moderate motivation to become better supervisors can benefit from the competition and modeling by teachers who are enthusiastic and resourceful in completing their assignments.

As part of the training we suggest at least 20 hours of practice. The first five to ten observations (which can be 20 to 30 minutes in duration) should be strictly to gain experience with several different observation techniques such as at task, selective verbatim, interaction patterns, and classroom movement. Teachers are usually willing to let a colleague practice his or her newly acquired skills in their classrooms. They are usually interested in seeing the data even though a feedback conference is not part of the assignment. When the observers feel confident, then planning and feedback should be added as part of the assignment. Observers who are practicing these new skills are often rewarded by the response they get from teachers who find the systematic observational records to be interesting and relevant.

# Notes

1. Portions of this chapter are adapted from Keith A. Acheson, "The Principal's Role in Instructional Leadership," *OSSC Bulletin* 28, No. 8 (April 1985); and Keith A. Acheson with Stuart C. Smith, "It Is Time for Principals to Share the Responsibility for Instructional Leadership with Others," *OSSC Bulletin* 29, No. 6 (February 1986). Both were prepared by the ERIC Clearinghouse on Educational Management for the Oregon School Study Council, University of Oregon, Eugene. ERIC/CEM is funded by the U.S. Department of Education. Additional portions are adapted from Keith A. Acheson, "A Central Role for Principals," *OSSC Report* 23, No. 3 (Spring 1983), developed under contract with the Northwest Regional Educational Laboratory and reproduced by permission of the laboratory.

2. Thomas I. Ellis, "Teacher Competency: What Administrators Can Do," *ERIC Digest*, No. 9 (Eugene, OR: ERIC Clearinghouse on Educational Management, 1984).

3. Arthur E. Wise, Linda Darling-Hammond, Milbrey W. McLaughlin, Harriet T. Bernstein: *Teacher Evaluation: A Study of Effective Practices*. Prepared for the National Institute of Education, June 1984, The Rand Corporation, Santa Monica, California; Milbrey Wallin McLaughlin, "Teacher Evaluation and School Improvement," *Teachers College Record* 86, No. 1 (Fall 1984).

4. Edwin Bridges, *Managing the Incompetent Teacher* (Eugene, OR: The ERIC Clearinghouse on Educational Management, 1984).

5. JoAnn Mazzarella, "The Principal's Role as an Instructional Leader," *ACSA School Management Digest*, Ser. 1, No. 3 (1977).

6. Roland Barth, "The Principal as Staff Developer," *Journal of Education* 163 (Spring 1981): 144–62.

7. Paul Hershey and Kenneth Blanchard, *Management of Organizational Behavior: Utilizing Human Resources* (Englewood Cliffs, NJ: Prentice-Hall, 1982).

8. H. S. Broudy, "Didactics, Heuristics, and Philetics," *Educational Theory* 22 (Summer 1972): 251–61. Can also be found in Ronald Hyman, *Teaching: Vantage Points for Study* (New York: J. B. Lippincott, 1974).

9. G. Polya, *How to Solve It* (Princeton, NJ: Princeton University Press, 1971).

10. Douglas MacGregor, *The Human Side of Enterprise* (New York: McGraw-Hill, 1960).

11. Theodore Parsons, *Guided Self-Analysis System for Professional Development Education Series* (Berkeley: University of California Press, 1968).

12. For principals who feel maligned by our skepticism, let us admit that we do not have data on *all* principals, or even *most*, but if the few thousand we have met or the several thousand whose teachers have responded to our surveys are representative, then we feel justified in stating that

*many* principals do not treat instructional leadership as their prime concern, except in response to questionnaires.

13. B. R. Joyce and B. Showers, "The Coaching of Teaching," *Educational Leadership* 40 (October 1982): 4–10; Beverly Showers, "Teachers Coaching Teachers," *Educational Leadership* 42 (April 1985): 43–48.

# Answers to Multiple-Choice Questions

### Unit One

1*c*, 2*d*, 3*a*, 4*b*, 5*a*, 6*c*, 7*d*, 8*d*, 9*d*, 10*c*

### Unit Two

1*e*; 2*e*; 3*c, e*; 4*e*; 5*a, b, c*; 6*e*; 7*e*; 8*a, d*

### Unit Three

1*d*, 2*c*, 3*b*, 4*c*, 5*a*, 6*c*, 7*a*, 8*d*, 9*b*, 10*d*

### Unit Four

1*c*; 2*d*; 3*b*; 4*e*; 5*c, d*; 6*a, e*; 7*d*; 8*c, e*

# Answers to Problems

## Unit One

1. The supervisor might begin by acknowledging the teacher's distress (technique 27), then ask the teacher to clarify why she is distressed (technique 28). If the teacher states that she feels her teaching is inadequate, the supervisor might initiate a clinical supervision cycle in which observation data are collected to help the teacher objectively analyze her teaching. If the teacher's distress is caused by personal problems, the supervisor might assume a counselor role (see pages 16, 17) or refer the teacher to an expert source of help.

2. The supervisor might enlarge on the question by discussing all supervisory roles with the student teacher. If the supervisor's roles are both to evaluate the student teacher's performance and to help the student improve in skill, the supervisor might discuss both roles and how they relate to each other (see pages 18–19). A supervisor who has an evaluative role might allay some of the student teacher's concerns by sharing the criteria that will be used to evaluate the student teacher's effectiveness (see pages 40–49).

3. It may well be true that, *to an extent*, good teachers are born, not made. Nevertheless, there is strong evidence that a teacher's classroom performance can be improved, *to an extent*, through training (see pages 23, 24). Also, it may be true that certain aspects of effective teaching will always elude technical analysis. But most educators (including critics of analytic methods) can identify *some* teaching techniques that differentiate effective and ineffective teachers. In other words, a possible problem with both claims is that they are too extreme.

## Unit Two

1, 2. Answers will, of course, vary. Share your answer with a friend.

3. Answers will vary but should attend to

   *a.* the kind of lesson you will teach
   *b.* what you, as teacher, will do
   *c.* what the students will do
   *d.* the concern, goal, or focus you have chosen
   *e.* the kinds of data you will collect

## Unit Three

1. Techniques that focus on specific behaviors, such as selective verbatim and at task, are probably inappropriate in this situation. You might consider instead a wide-lens technique—for example, an anecdotal record or a video or audio recording. Although more restricted, Flanders Interaction Analysis also may be helpful. These techniques enable a teacher to examine his or her teaching behavior and how students react to it. In examining these records, the teacher may develop a better operational definition of what is meant by "coming across."

2. An at-task analysis would be helpful in determining the percentage of time that each of these students is engaged in learning and the percentage of time that they are off task. Off-task time can be analyzed further into several categories of behavior (e.g., daydreaming, chatting with a classmate). The supervisor might also make an anecdotal record limited to the target students and the teacher's interaction with them. Another observational technique that may be appropriate is a selective verbatim in which the supervisor records all teacher comments directed to the problem student.

3. *Inferences*

   *a.* Students near the front of the room do more talking than students in the back of the room.
   *b.* Most of the teacher's questions are addressed to the class as a whole rather than to specific students.
   *c.* A higher proportion of girls than boys responded to the teacher.
   *d.* Several students engaged in conversations with each other while the lesson was in progress.
   *e.* Almost half the students (10 of 21) did not participate in the lesson.

*Recommendations*

a. Have students in the back of the room move into empty seats nearer the front of the room.

b. The teacher should consider standing so that she has a good view of all students.

c. If side conversations between students persist, the teacher should explain why this behavior is not desirable or perhaps should move some students to different sections of the room.

d. Direct more questions to specific students rather than to the class as a whole.

4. *Selective verbatim of feedback statements*

All right.

A couple of billion.

Six million.

Only a billion.

About three billion.

All right, Mary is closest because it is over three billion people in the world today.

All right, there are a lot of people that are just barely making it.

**Timeline coding**

## Unit Four

1. *a.* Alternatives will vary. Individual conferences with students are usually better than public rebukes. Attention to planning productive activities to replace negative behavior is advisable. Reinforcing prositive behavior is a powerful tool. There are many other reasonable suggestions.

*b.* "If I were you, here's what I would try" is not a good opener.

"Here are several possibilities; can you suggest others?" is better.

2. Responses will vary depending on the nature of the strategy chosen. Have you considered photographs, checklists, student feedback (questionnaires, reports, evaluations), getting assistance from student teachers, aides, or others?

3. The following examples for student behavior are from Spaulding. The examples for teacher conference behavior are from our own experience; the list can easily be expanded.

Aggressive Behavior—direct verbal or physical attack, grabbing, destroying:
  "Give me that!"
  "Get out of my room!"
Negative (Inappropriate) Attention-Getting Behavior—annoying, bothering, belittling, criticizing:
  "You don't know how to jump rope."
  "You've never had to teach a class like this one."
Manipulating and Directing Others:
  "Tell Cynthia to get out of the wagon."
  "You ought to spend your time on kids, not teachers."
Resisting Authority (or Delaying):
  "No, I won't do it!"
  "Would you mind repeating the question?"
Self-Directed Activity:
  "I think I'll make a pie."
  "I'd like to make some tape recordings on my own."
Paying Rapt Attention:
  Listening attentively as teacher gives directions
  Watching supervisor give demonstration lesson
Sharing and Helping:
  Child eagerly takes part in activity or conversation
  Teacher suggests alternative teaching activities
Transacting:
  Mutual give-and-take is present in (child's) activities
Seeking Help:
  "Would you help me fix this?"
  "What would *you* do?"
Following Directions (Passively and Submissively):
  Doing assigned work without enthusiasm or great interest
  Trying the supervisor's suggestion for a class activity, but with a lack of zest

Seeking or Responding to External Stimuli:
    Observing passively, easily diverted
    Listening impassively and attending to any interruption
Responding to Internal Stimuli:
    Daydreaming
    Gazing into the distance
Physical Withdrawal or Avoidance:
    Moving away from teacher and other children
    Missing the conference appointment

# Index

**Keith Acheson** received his Ed.D. in Curriculum and Instruction from Stanford University in 1964. He has taught and is Professor of Education at the University of Oregon. He has been active in federal programs such as Teacher Corps, regional laboratories, and research and development centers. He is Associate Director of the ERIC Clearinghouse on Educational Management.

**Meredith Gall** received his Ph.D. in psychology from the University of California at Berkeley in 1968. From 1968 to 1974 he was Senior Program Associate at the Far West Laboratory for Educational Research and Development, where he was active in the design of teacher education programs and in research on teaching. Since 1975 he has been a professor in the Department of Curriculum and Instruction at the University of Oregon. He has published extensively in the areas of staff development, teaching methods, and instructional improvement. He is coauthor, with Walter Borg, of *Educational Research*, fourth edition, also published by Longman Inc.